SURVIVE

AND

THRIVE

120 IDEAS TO CULTIVATE YOUR LEADERSHIP AGILITY

ANDREW WILLIAMS

INDEPENDENT INK

First published 2019 by Independent Ink
PO Box 1638, Carindale
Queensland 4152 Australia
independentink.com.au

Cover design by Maria Biaggini

Edited by Rebecca Hamilton

Internal design by Independent Ink
Typeset in 11.5/15.6 pt Adobe Garamond by Post Pre-press Group, Brisbane

A catalogue record for this
book is available from the
National Library of Australia
NATIONAL
LIBRARY
OF AUSTRALIA

ISBN 978-0-6485548-0-6 (paperback)
ISBN 978-0-6485548-1-3 (epub)
ISBN 978-0-6485548-2-0 (kindle)

Disclaimer:
Names and identifying details have been changed to protect the privacy of individuals and businesses. Any information in the book is purely the opinion of the author based on personal experience and should not be taken as business or legal advice. All material is provided for educational purposes only. We recommend to always seek the advice of a qualified professional before making any decision regarding personal and business needs.

CONTENTS

INTRODUCTION

The Business Case for Leadership Agility 1

The Six Rules of Thumb for Leadership Agility. 7

THINKING DIFFERENTLY

Chapter 1   Reflective Practice 13

Chapter 2   Enhance Your Sense Making 19

Chapter 3   Reflection in Action (The Balcony and the
Dancefloor). 24

Chapter 4   Adopt a Growth Mindset 29

Chapter 5   Understand Your Context. 35

Chapter 6   Make Conflictual Interpretations of Your Context . . 40

Chapter 7   Become a Systems Thinker. 45

Chapter 8   Embrace Dualities. 51

Chapter 9   Demonstrate Curiosity 57

Chapter 10 Practice Mindfulness 63

Chapter 11 Manage Your Cognitive Biases 69

ENGAGING DIFFERENTLY

Chapter 12 Build Leadership Density 79

Chapter 13 Creating Psychological Safety. 85

Chapter 14 Deep Listening 90

Chapter 15 Be Trustworthy 95

Chapter 16 Develop Empathy. 100

Chapter 17 Embrace a Different Perspective 107

Chapter 18 Embrace Productive Conflict. 113

Chapter 19 Embrace your Vulnerability 119

Chapter 20 Engage with Generative Dialogue 125

Chapter 21 Understand your Stakeholders' World 128

ACTING DIFFERENTLY

Chapter 22 Move Out of Your Comfort Zone and
Into Your Learning Zone 135

Chapter 23 Be an Experimenter 140

Chapter 24 Let Simple Rules Guide You 145

Chapter 25 Know Your Purpose 150

Chapter 26 Don't Overuse Your Strengths................. 155

Chapter 27 Give Up (Some) Control....................... 160

Chapter 28 Diversify Your Experiences.................... 165

Chapter 29 Increase Your Understanding of Self . . . Through
the Eyes of Others 171

Chapter 30 Open Yourself Up to Feedback................. 177

Chapter 31 Make Progress On Your Own Personal Adaptive
Challenge 182

Chapter 32 Institute Your Own 90-Day Plan (And Weekly Plan). . 188

Chapter 33 Understand Your Emotional Triggers............ 194

Chapter 34 Manage Your Emotions....................... 201

Chapter 35 Unleash Your Creativity....................... 206

Chapter 36 Decision Agility............................... 211

Final Thoughts................................... 217

Acknowledgements.............................. 219

About the Author 221

References 223

The Business Case for Leadership Agility

On a recent leadership agility workshop I was facilitating, the participants were discussing how they were personally impacted by complexity in their lives. They had many stories about dealing with the rapidness of change, cultural differences, information overload, diverse stakeholder needs, and handling current demands while transforming their business to cope with the future. Then Richie spoke up.

I could tell Richie was someone who the group listened to deeply. He agreed with everything that had been said, and opened up about the complexities in his personal life. He spoke with vulnerability about his homelife, where he and his partner were raising three children – one with a disability, one starting school, and one being a newborn. Both parents were working and had little in the way of logistical support due to their location.

This started a conversation amongst the group about how complexity in their personal lives exacerbated complexity in their professional lives. Richie's story really highlighted something we all innately know to be true: operating in complexity is tough. In order to thrive, we must be open and agile, and ready to respond to the curve balls that our professional and personal lives throw at us.

This is why I chose to write this book, and why I hope you have chosen to read it. We are all experiencing rapid change and facing new challenges, and our existing personal 'hardware' won't be enough to survive, let alone thrive.

So what are some of these challenges?

Organisations, like those of many of my clients, are facing a new world of challenges – such as the increasing globalisation of the marketplace and the threat of new entrants, uncertainty around energy policy and the focus on alternative energy sources, changing customer expectations, and accelerated innovation. Emerging technologies such as artificial intelligence, robotics and machine learning are developing at a rapid rate and leading to widespread changes in the workplace. Organisations are impacted as they balance their need for growth with the need for reskilling workers whose jobs may be at risk of becoming obsolete.

We are also seeing significant change in how organisations engage with their people, communities and society. It is not enough to focus on growth and profit; there is now a higher expectation of the broader contribution that organisations make to society as a whole.

Profit before people doesn't cut it anymore. The 2019 Financial Services Royal Commission report in Australia highlighted what happens when an industry doesn't meet their moral obligations.

As a result there have been wholesale changes in banking, with senior executives leaving and significant investment in cultural transformation to meet customer and community expectations. A positive example of where Australian organisations took a leadership role at a societal level was the same-sex marriage debate in 2017. At the time you could argue the public was disappointed in the role the government played in leading this debate, and the business community (the BCA and CEOs of some of Australia's largest organisations) stepped in to show leadership through their policies, lobbying and influence. Alan Joyce comes to mind as someone who advocated for same-sex marriage in his position as Qantas CEO – even under criticism from Peter Dutton, a senior government minister. This is an example of where organisations understood the community sentiment and acted accordingly.

Digital transformation is also rapidly changing the way customers connect with businesses. In order to keep up and stay competitive, organisations must adjust to these demands by digitising their processes and business models. Many businesses have already begun this transition as they realise they cannot be left behind. Those that don't adapt are destined to end up in the corporate graveyard, along with other notable organisations like Blockbuster, Kodak, Sears and Borders.

The rise of new technologies has also led to changes in the labour market, with the growth of the gig economy, where the traditional worker–employee relationship is being transformed by the proliferation of freelancers and contractors. Recently I lived and worked in Bali and was staggered by the amount of co-working spaces and the entrepreneurial nomads inhabiting them. These freelancers and business-owners typically wouldn't have been any older than 30. And I don't think this phenomenon is specific to only Bali. Some quick research highlighted that co-working spaces have grown significantly across Asia, Africa, Latin America and the subcontinent. The growth in the number of digital nomads, co-working spaces and the gig economy has implications for how organisations and their leaders manage culture, engagement, and how they attract and develop talent.

Beyond the world of business, we also have changes at a political and societal level, such as Brexit, the nationalist agenda of American politics and the advancement of rights for minority groups. These changes provide further challenges, requiring organisations to be nimble, agile and willing to adapt.

The complexity of the changing environment in which organisations find themselves has increased rapidly over the past few years. An environment that is complex is one that features many connecting parts, multiple key decision factors and diverse stakeholders. Additionally, there is an overwhelming amount of information available, and the problems and challenges that organisations face are likely to be systemic with no obvious cause and effect.

Organisations need to find new ways to compete and survive in this complex world, yet many of the workforces upon whose expertise success has previously been built find themselves stuck and unable to innovate or move away from the historical definitions of their business and operating models. Traditional leadership characteristics of directive and siloed approaches need to make way for something more collaborative, where the collective can enable and deliver a move to the new.

The challenge for organisations today and tomorrow is how to cultivate a workforce that is nimble, responsive and collaborative in approach, and able to foster new thinking and ideas with ease. This was confirmed in a 2015 *Harvard Business Review* report[1] on the critical competencies needed for leadership success in times of complexity. Through interviews with their clients and reviewing leadership research, the authors found that personal adaptability and learning from experience were key capabilities needed to navigate complexity. They highlighted that 'leaders who demonstrate personal adaptability remain focused and effective in the face of uncertainty and ambiguity. They also tend to be highly resilient . . . research highlighted that personal adaptability was highly correlated with leadership effectiveness.'[2]

Many of my clients are noticing a world that is far more challenging than what they are used to. They share experiences of feeling overwhelmed with information and data, of being unable to predict the future and of feeling out of their depth. They are all seeking to be more agile in this complex world, and my work is about giving them the necessary tools, guidance and compassion to achieve that goal.

I define leadership agility as 'the capacity to think, engage and act *differently* to survive and thrive in a rapidly complex and changing world'. I have purposefully emphasised the word differently. We have to *be* different if we want to adapt. If we continue to use the same comfortable approaches to situations, we risk staying stagnant and not making progress. Agility requires us to be bold and to extend ourselves beyond our comfort zones.

This is what this book is about.

I have had the privilege of working in a range of organisations in different industries and with thousands of leaders through individual and team coaching, speaking engagements, feedback sessions and workshops. I have drawn upon their experiences and the work I have done with them to help frame the contents of this book. I have also been inspired by Jennifer Garvey Berger and her work on cultivating leadership. Her white paper,[3] co-authored with Catherine Fitzgerald, titled 'Coaching for an Increasingly Complex World', inspired the structure of this book, which is broken into three parts: Thinking Differently, Engaging Differently and Acting Differently. Within each part there are a series of chapters with a number of practical ideas that you can easily put in place to help increase your leadership agility.

The first section is about thinking differently, and it covers topics such as adopting a growth mindset, understanding the impact of cognitive biases, being a systems thinker and increasing your sense making.

The second section is about engaging differently with others, and it covers topics such as building leadership density, understanding your stakeholders' world, embracing vulnerability and practicing deep listening.

The third section is about acting differently, and it includes topics such as managing your emotions, opening yourself up to feedback, becoming an experimenter and giving up control.

This book is not an academic book, nor was it intended to be. It's a practical guide to help cultivate your capacity to cope with greater complexity, and to be agile and adaptable in doing so. Everything that is suggested is supported by evidence and research from a range of brilliant thinkers, as well as my own client experiences. What I have been able to do is synthesise that evidence and research with my own experiences into, I hope, a coherent and accessible book.

You can read the book cover-to-cover, if that's your thing, but by no means do you have to approach it this way. I like to see it as a book where you can apply the rules of thumb on a daily basis (see opposite) and then simply dip back in when you are looking for some more guidance or help with thinking, engaging and acting differently.

I hope you enjoy reading this book, and that it makes a difference in both your professional and personal life.

The Six Rules of Thumb for Leadership Agility

I like having rules of thumb to help me operate in my world. Rules of thumb are simple principles or habits that you put in place to better manage your context. In this case, the context is how to be agile in times of complexity and rapid change.

I have identified six rules of thumb to help simplify your complex world. If you can incorporate these simple rules into your leadership practice, you give yourself a good chance of exercising good leadership, no matter what comes your way:

1. Understand yourself and how others experience you.
2. Play outside your comfort zone. Get comfortable with being uncomfortable.
3. Embrace a learning and growth mindset in everything you do.
4. Interpret your context with curiosity, honesty and accountability.
5. Build leadership density.
6. Experiment, reflect, make sense and repeat.

Each one of these rules of thumb is explained in more detail below.

1. **Understand yourself and how others experience you.** In your professional and personal life, others will experience the impact of your behaviours and not your intentions. Focus on

how others experience you and not just how you see yourself. Seek feedback, don't be too hard on yourself, and get more effective aligning your intentions with impact.

2. **Play outside your comfort zone. Get comfortable with being uncomfortable.** That's where the magic of learning and growth happens. Look for experiences that stretch you, challenge and even scare you, and lean into them. When I ask people about their most memorable or impactful development experience, they talk about the pressure, stress and challenges. They also talk about having no option other than to learn. The more you play outside your comfort zone, the more likely you will learn and grow. This growth helps us to be more agile and adaptable.

3. **Embrace a learning and growth mindset in everything you do.** It is impossible to fail if you have a learning mindset because every mistake or loss is an opportunity for growth. If you are struggling when you are outside your comfort zone, simply ask yourself, what am I meant to be learning here? Those who have agility have an extraordinary commitment to learning. I don't mean technical learning, but the learning of new behaviours, mindsets and belief systems.

4. **Interpret your context with curiosity, honesty and accountability.** In a complex environment or context, don't fall for the trap of responding quickly with the first solution. You need to interpret your context with curiosity and honesty. What is truly happening? What are we missing? What is systemic here? Don't be blinded by your own perspective; get others to provide their perspective and keep it real. Invest time in what you are seeing.

5. **Build leadership density.** Responding to complexity requires all of us to exercise leadership. Help build leadership density

(where everyone feels the power to contribute) amongst many, and not the few. Create an environment where anyone can exercise leadership at any time. This overturns the hero model of leadership where power is centred with the few. To operate in complexity you need the collective to be successful.

6. **Experiment, reflect, make sense and repeat.** If there's one thing I have learnt over the years, it's the importance of experimentation. In every coaching session, I encourage my clients to think of small experiments that they can learn from. If we want to operate in a complex environment and make progress, then we need to experiment to see what works and what doesn't. Try things, run small experiments that may fail, take small steps, learn from them, experiment again, and repeat!

These rules of thumb are further expanded upon throughout this book, with a special focus in Chapter 24. Make these rules of thumb part of your leadership practice, and give yourself every opportunity to be the best leader you can be.

THINKING DIFFERENTLY

If we are to successfully navigate the challenges we face in our complex world, then our current thinking won't be enough. This reminds me of a quote (mistakenly) credited to Einstein: 'Problems cannot be solved by the same level of thinking that created them.' We also need to give ourselves space to think, as our bias for action impedes quality thinking.

In each workshop I run, the first thing I talk to participants about, regardless of their professional background, is reflective practice. Reflective practice is a way of embedding a learning mindset. It encourages individuals to observe their experiences, make sense of them, and experiment with new ways of thinking and behaving. In my work, I notice that those who have a well-developed reflective practice are better able to see the limitations of their current ways of thinking and are more willing to experiment.

Those who think differently are willing to interrogate their environment with honesty. They are able to distinguish between adaptive and technical challenges (see pages 35–36). They are comfortable with ambiguity and paradox, and are not governed by a sense of urgency or a bias for action. They avoid black-and-white thinking and know that showing curiosity and asking questions opens them up to new possibilities.

In this section I will delve into some of the practices that will help you think differently. These include understanding the context in which you operate (Chapter 5), sense making (Chapter 2), embracing dualities (Chapter 8) and practicing mindfulness (Chapter 10).

CHAPTER 1

Reflective Practice

Leadership agility is about continuously learning, and one way to approach this is through reflective practice.

Reflective practice is so important I have made it a rule of thumb (number 6). It involves learning from your experiences and applying the insights you gain to similar or different experiences. A simple but effective definition I like to use is: 'Reflective practice encompasses intentionally reflecting on your actions and experiences, making sense of them, and implementing changes with a view to continuously learn and grow.'

There are a number of different models or frameworks that help us understand reflective practice. In this chapter, I will focus on a standard approach to reflective practice. In Chapter 3, titled 'Reflection in Action', I will focus on a dynamic real-time approach using the metaphor of 'The Balcony and Dancefloor' – a concept developed by leadership expert Ron Heifetz.

Each day is filled with experiences – some of them small (sending emails or taking phone calls), some of them big (losing a contract with a longstanding client or winning a new job). In our personal life it is the same.

In each of these experiences, there are opportunities for growth. Some of us, however, let those opportunities pass. Some of us are happy to simply live the experience rather than reflect on how that experience could help us learn and grow.

There are three types of learners that I come across in my work, each with a different approach to reflective practice:

1. **Blocked.** Blocked learners resist learning from experiences. They tend to make the same mistakes repeatedly. They often blame factors that are external to themselves if things go wrong, but are happy claiming responsibility when things go well. They either lack the willingness or the capacity to learn from their experiences.

2. **Passive.** Passive learners have some degree of reflective practice but don't translate their reflections into actions. I see many passive learners in my leadership programs. They have great intentions to take their learning back into the workplace but, when they get there, the busyness takes over and not much changes.

3. **Active.** Active learners embody reflective practice. They are open to new experiences and see them as an opportunity to learn. Their learning radars are always making observations and identifying insights, and, most importantly, they put their insights and learnings into practice. In my workshops, feedback sessions and coaching, active learners demonstrate qualities such as self-awareness, curiosity, a questioning mindset, and a willingness to take ownership of their learning.

In my work, I spend time helping those who are 'passive' learners to become 'active' learners. Implementing good reflective practice is a way of doing this.

So, what does this reflective practice look like?

My approach to reflective practice is based closely on Kolb's learning cycle.[4] There are four stages in the reflective practice:

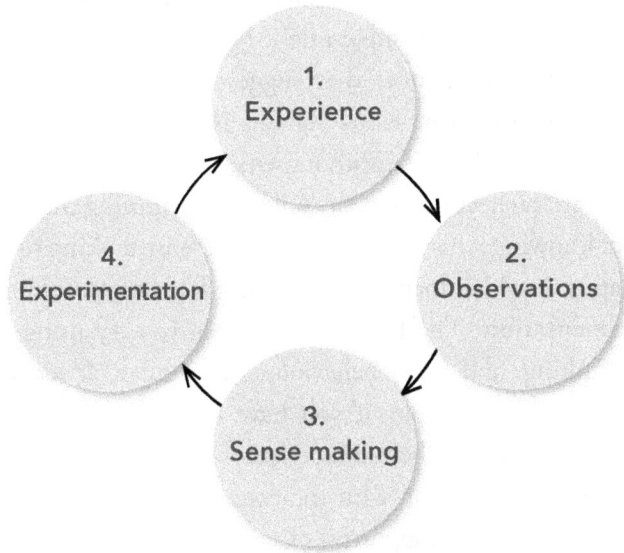

1. **Experience.** This is the active involvement in a task or activity. It can include any type of experience, such as an email exchange with a peer, a presentation to a leadership team or a conflict with a key stakeholder in the organisation.

2. **Observations.** This step involves developing awareness of your experience, stepping back and reviewing what is working and what is not working. It may include talking with others about what happened in your experience, identifying your behaviours as well as your emotional reactions to the experience. There is no judgement in the observation stage, just an objective collection of data.

3. **Sense making.** This step involves making sense of, or taking meaning from, your observations. In this stage, individuals look for insights and learning, with a focus on developing new ways of thinking and behaving. They learn to identify patterns,

connect the dots and better understand what happened in their experience. An example might be a pattern you identify from multiple experiences that suggests you withdraw from conflictual experiences. Knowing this is a pattern allows you to do something about it. Without sense making the experience becomes an intellectual exercise. A little like winning the lottery and not knowing what money is! I discuss sense making further in Chapter 2, which includes an example from my coaching.

4. **Experimentation.** The final stage is when you try using your new thinking and new behaviours in similar or different experiences. For example, if you have identified a pattern of withdrawing from conflictual experiences, you might experiment by having a conversation with someone who you have conflict with, but who is also supportive of you. It might be easier than experimenting with someone who is extremely difficult. I also discuss experiments in more detail in Chapter 23.

Each of these four stages of reflective practice are important, and you need to work through each stage rather than rush to an experiment. Making observations and identifying insights are a vital part of the reflective practice process.

Agile leaders make reflective practice an integral part of the daily practice. Without reflective practice and a commitment to learning, adaptability and agility are virtually impossible.

Ideas for developing your reflective practice

Journaling

One great way to develop your reflective practice is to journal your experience. In fact, you might like to go beyond that and keep a journal where you document daily your experiences, your observations and your insights. Since I started my improv comedy classes I've been keeping a journal, and after every class and performance I document my observations, learning and feedback from my teacher. I have noticed my confidence building as I start to experiment and action the feedback I am given. Journaling helps you get out of your linear and sequential thinking, and enables you to take a big picture view of your feelings, observations and insights. It allows you to identify patterns in your behaviour from a detached perspective.

You don't have to be a world-class writer to keep a journal. Just start writing. Step back and, with a third-person perspective, look for insights and learning. When you run your experiments, document your results. You might be pleasantly surprised by the results.

So, don't hesitate; start a journal! You can use a nice moleskin, or a playful diary from Typo, or even the notes section or an app on your phone.

Peer coaching

I ask peers to help with my reflective practice, particularly when I am in the sense-making stage. I spend time sharing my experiences and observations, and I encourage them to challenge me around making sense of them. This third-person view helps me to see things that I may not if I am working through the process by myself. Identify a couple of peers who you trust and who think differently to you, and ask them to help you make sense of your experiences. The most important thing is to be open to being challenged by the person.

Commit to the practice

My experience of people who are very good learners is that they commit to the practice of reflection. This is a signature skill of the active learners that I mentioned earlier in this chapter. I suggest carrying around your journal (or your phone if you use the notes section or an app) at all times and using on-the-go opportunities, such as commuting or walking to your next meeting, to reflect on your experience. What is important is that you integrate those on-the-go notes into your more formal practice. One practice that I adopt is taking time each evening to document my observations and insights from the day, as well as what I am grateful for. You may not want to do it every day, but having a regular practice will ensure a noticeable difference in how you see the world.

CHAPTER 2

Enhance Your Sense Making

In the previous chapter, I discussed the importance of reflective practice. Consisting of four key steps – experience, observation, sense making and observation – reflective practice creates a learning mindset, which enables continual growth. This chapter goes into more depth regarding the sense making component of the reflection process.

So, what exactly is sense making?

It's about deriving meaning from what we observe and experience. It helps us interpret the data we collect, and navigate ambiguity and uncertainty in an ongoing effort to understand connections and develop situational awareness. If we can make sense of the world we operate in, we can choose to respond more effectively.

You can employ sense making with any experience. This may include a meeting with your manager, a project you worked on that didn't go well or an interaction with a stakeholder.

Let me illustrate through an example from my coaching. Tom was a General Manager who wanted to be more influential with stakeholders, whether they be his peers, managers or key internal customers. In one of our early sessions, Tom relayed his experience of a meeting he had with his peers and his manager. Collectively they were debating the implementation of an important project that Tom was leading. Tom had identified some risks in implementing the project, but was getting pushback from his colleagues who were keen to see the project move forward. The more he tried to outline his case in the meeting, the more resistance he encountered. The group made concession on one of his ideas, but, overall, he felt steamrolled.

In our coaching session, we talked about what happened and, more importantly, how to make sense of what happened so that he could make changes that would enable him to be more successful in the future.

Through a series of questions about his experience, as well as similar experiences in the past, we were able to gain insight into what went wrong in the meeting. The contributing factors included his focus on logic when arguing his perspective, the less effective relationship he had with a couple of key influential peers, and the tendency to withdraw when he felt what he said 'didn't matter' to others. Tom realised that he did withdraw when he felt his perspective was not being taken into account. He noted that this was a pattern for him across a broad range of experiences. He also noted that he was data driven and logical when arguing a case, and had not invested time into key relationships amongst his peers. Tom recognised he was outcome-focused rather than relational, and came to understand, via our sense making, that his peers could see that. Essentially, what was happening in the meeting was a microcosm of what was happening outside the meeting, both professionally and personally.

Sense making in Tom's situation, and indeed in any situation, can be done through questions and reflection. These questions can include:

▶ If my peers or manager were here, what would they say happened?

▶ What's my 'stuff' in this experience? Or how do my faulty beliefs and assumptions contribute to this experience?

▶ What data am I missing? What additional information would be helpful here?

▶ Has this happened before? What are the patterns that I am seeing?

▶ Where do these patterns show up beyond this context?

▶ If I were to provide three interpretations of this experience, what would they be?

▶ What stops me from choosing a different response?

▶ What am I most afraid of?

▶ What am I most excited about?

▶ What is my belief here?

▶ How certain are my conclusions? Where might I be wrong?

▶ What would my coach say?

▶ What is my learning here?

Sense making is not easy to do by ourselves. One of the challenges we face when interpreting what we see is unknowingly laying our own biases and world view over the top of it. In other words, we create a perspective that may be different to the actual reality that is occurring. If we want to make sense of a situation, we need to challenge our thinking, and the best way to do that is to engage someone who thinks differently in a conversation. This might be a coach, as they are usually well trained in asking questions that help their clients make sense of an experience. If you don't have access to a coach, then use a respected and trustworthy peer, mentor or a friend.

Once you have managed to make sense of your experience, and create insights and meaning, then the next important step is to integrate new ideas and behaviours into future experiences. This is discussed further in Chapter 23 on experiments.

Ideas for enhancing your sense making

Rewind the tape

One of the techniques I use to help people make sense of their experience is asking them to 'rewind the tape' and identify what is happening from an objective standpoint. I might ask the question: 'If someone was watching as an observer, what would they be seeing?' Doing this alone would constitute a technique in the observation step of reflective practice; discussing it with a coach or peer pushes it into sense-making territory. I find that the act of 'rewinding the tape' and objectively sharing what I am seeing helps accelerate my insights and sense making. Sometimes I have to 'rewind the tape' on some of the TV shows I watch. I often miss something in the first viewing, and rewinding allows me to pick what I may have missed earlier. Watching movies for a second (or sometimes third) time helps me see things that I might have missed in the first viewing. I had to watch *Get Out* by Jordan Peele three times to fully make sense of that movie!

Journal your experience

As mentioned in the previous chapter, journaling can be incredibly helpful in reflective practice. Just let your thoughts and feelings emerge on the page, then try and answer two or three of the questions listed in this chapter to help make sense of the experience. These questions get you in the mindset of learning and deepening your understanding of what is taking place.

Show yourself compassion

Sense making can often evoke feelings of failure and disappointment. A realisation that your emotional triggers were pushed when a conversation went off the rails, or disappointment that you recognised a pattern in your behaviour can make you feel vulnerable. The point of sense making is not to be hard on yourself or give data to your inner critic! Sense making is about self-awareness and learning what you can do differently as a result of your insights. So go easy on yourself.

CHAPTER 3

Reflection in Action
(The Balcony and the Dancefloor)

In the first chapter, I talked about reflective practice, where reflection and sense making happen after the experience. However, there is a dynamic process called 'reflection in action' where reflecting and action happen simultaneously in real time. This process also uses the metaphor of 'The Balcony and the Dancefloor', a concept developed by Ron Heifetz and Marty Linsky from the Harvard Kennedy School of Government.[5]

If you imagine being on a dancefloor, you are limited in what you see. You may see the person in front of you, how they are moving, what they are wearing, and maybe another person or two in your peripheral vision.

If you then imagine looking down onto the dancefloor from a balcony, you get a different perspective that is less limiting than your view from the dancefloor. You start to see the movement, the colours of what people are wearing, where there might be gaps in the dancefloor, the style of dancing, and people moving on and off the dancefloor. You have a far broader view from above.

The only challenge with being on the balcony is that you are not part of the dancing experience. You are an observer only and you are unable to intervene (make a contribution). You need to move from the balcony to the dancefloor to contribute and make a difference. Reflection in action requires you to move from observation and interpretation (balcony) to intervention and action (dancefloor).

How might this play out in your life? Imagine you are in a challenging conversation with your colleague. You are both arguing your perspective about the lack of collaboration between your two teams. This challenging conversation is happening on the dancefloor. You are both 'in action' through the conversation you are having. You switch up to the balcony as you are having this conversation and start to observe several things. First, it is obvious to you that the conversation doesn't appear to be going well. You notice that the tone is adversarial, and neither of you are listening to each other. You observe that both of you are trying to assert your opinion without trying to understand the other's perspective. At this stage, you can't do anything about it because you are still on the balcony. You have to go back to the dancefloor and make an intervention. This might be as simple as naming and sharing your observations. You may say to your colleague, 'James, I feel as though we are not listening to each other and this is not helping us make progress on this issue. How can we change the dynamic of this conversation in a way that helps both of us?'

This intervention based on your observation has the potential to change the conversation for the better. Another intervention might involve you ceasing to assert your view and starting to role model a better way to have the conversation.

Whichever approach you choose, your intervention will be based on an observation you made from the balcony. Getting up on the balcony involves observation and sense making, and going back down to the dancefloor involves intervention and experimentation.

The ability to shift seamlessly between reflection, insight and action enables you to be agile in the moment. This is an incredibly powerful technique to use.

The diagram below sets out this process.

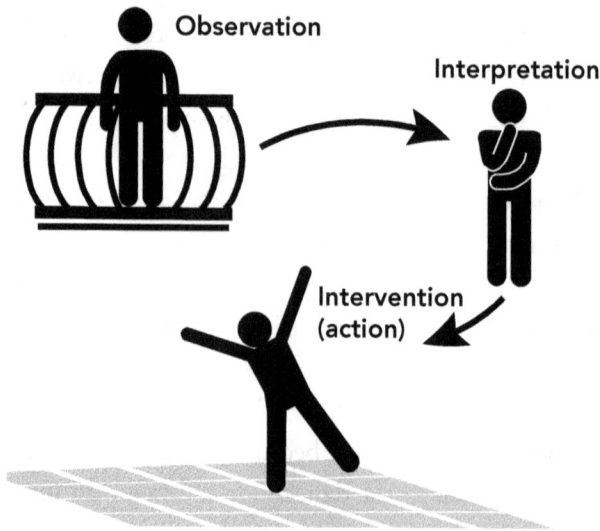

Reflection in action can be useful at any time. Other situations might include team meetings or a group discussion. If the group discussion feels awkward or tense, you might observe that the group is avoiding an elephant in the room, so you might share that observation with the group. You may find that simply naming the elephant will enable you to have a real conversation and make progress as a group.

One other powerful way to use this technique is on yourself. For example, you may use this technique to observe your emotions or behaviours and work out why you're not speaking up in a meeting (or even speaking too much in a meeting). Notice the emotions you are experiencing when interacting with someone, or observe the mood or interest in the group when you are presenting to them.

I often use reflection in action when I am running a workshop. It enables me to tap into the engagement of the group and make interventions to keep the energy alive or to keep specific people interested.

The concept of the balcony and the dancefloor is incredibly helpful when you are feeling overwhelmed. It stops you from being hijacked by your emotions and allows for greater clarity, better decision making and enhanced ability to influence.

Ideas for employing 'reflection in action'

Be a 'first-class noticer'

If you want to be good at reflection in action, you have to be a great observer and notice things around you. Those who regularly practice getting up on the balcony have a knack for seeing things that others don't. They don't get caught up in the emotion of the situation; they have the ability to step back and notice things. They pick up on the patterns and dynamics that are happening in a group or any system that involves people (e.g. a relationship). They notice things such as how they are coming across in one-on-one interactions. They don't judge; they simply observe what's going on around them. You could develop your noticing skills by simply starting to observe what is novel when you are out for a walk or a run, or even in the car or on public transport on the way to work. When you are in a meeting, practice noticing things such as who has the power, who is talking, who is not etc. This practice will enhance your noticing skills.

Stay in the moment

One thing that impacts on someone's ability to practice reflection in action effectively is a bias for action. If we are busy and focused on action, then this can prevent us from observing and interpreting what's going on within us and around us. I encourage you to stay in the moment and be present and mindful. Practicing mindfulness helps you stay in the present and helps your brain to notice more around you. It is hard to get up on the balcony if you are not able to stay present. We will explore mindfulness in detail in Chapter 10.

Don't hide up there on the balcony

When I explain the concept of the balcony and dancefloor in my workshops, a number of people who tend to be quieter in group situations tell me they are spending time on the balcony observing. However, if you are always on the balcony, you are never on the dancefloor, and that's where the action and the opportunities to influence take place. Don't use the balcony as an excuse to not contribute to a group conversation or to avoid your own anxieties. There is nothing wrong with observing your emotions, but, if you want to have any influence, you need to be on the dancefloor. Moving simultaneously between the dancefloor and balcony deftly is the key.

CHAPTER 4

Adopt a Growth Mindset

The work of Stanford University professor Carol Dweck[6] has centred on the implicit assumptions we make about the malleability or changeability of our personal attributes, such as our intelligence and personality. These assumptions that we make are called 'mindsets'. You might remember the third rule of thumb on page 8: 'Embrace a learning and growth mindset in everything you do.' This rule of thumb is discussed in more detail in this chapter. As a note, I use the terms 'growth mindset' and 'learning mindset' interchangeably.

Dweck found that there are two possible types of mindsets. The first is a 'fixed mindset', where an individual's implicit assumption is that personal attributes are fixed and don't change. The second is a 'growth mindset', where an individual's implicit assumption is that personal attributes are changeable with effort and hard work.

An individual with a fixed mindset has a tendency to focus on being perfect and doing things effortlessly. They are likely to do things that make the most of their 'natural talent'. The downside of those with a fixed mindset is that their focus on being great and doing things they are naturally good at can also constrain them. They may avoid challenges, be sceptical around development and effort, and fear failure. In fact, failure and not being perfect is highly stressful for someone with a fixed mindset. One of the main reasons for this is that their success and talent is seen as personal – attributable to who they are.

However, the flipside of this is that anything that causes them to fail or where they are not being seen as brilliant is also seen as personal. In other words, if you are no good at something, then you will never be good at it and it should therefore be avoided. I come across this in my coaching where individuals will talk about how they avoid difficult conversations as they feel clunky initiating them, or how they won't put their hand up for a presentation because there are others who they perceive as better presenters.

They would much prefer to focus on what they are effortlessly good at whilst skilfully avoiding anything that presents a challenge or might see them fail. As Dweck puts it, 'In short, when people believe in fixed traits, they are always in danger of being measured by a failure.'[7]

An individual with a growth mindset focuses on learning from their experiences, both good and not so good, throwing themselves at challenges, focusing on their own improvement and realising that effort is an important part of the development process. They don't see success as innate, but see hard work, effort and development as the keys to success. Those with a growth mindset are more likely to see their initial capability as a starting point and something to build on. They look at failure and setbacks with a sense of curiosity rather than judgement. When they face a challenge, they are able to reframe it as a learning experience.

I have this saying: 'You cannot fail if you have a learning mindset.' It reminds me of my introduction to improv comedy. Our very first activity was to bow in front of the class and yell out in a loud voice, 'I have failed!' The rest of the class applauded wildly in appreciation. It's okay to fail, as long as you are experimenting and learning. This principle fits very much with having a growth or learning mindset. If you want to make progress, you have to have a growth mindset; it's nearly impossible when your mindset is fixed.

An individual with a fixed mindset will find it difficult to demonstrate leadership agility. They avoid challenges, and they are more likely to view setbacks and struggles as proof of a lack of innate talent. Leadership agility requires a sense of curiosity, an openness to learning, and a willingness to undertake challenges that move us outside our comfort zone. Those with a fixed mindset tend to stay in their comfort zone, and see challenge and effort as something to avoid, whereas those with a growth mindset continually push themselves outside their comfort zone, and see challenge as an opportunity to learn and grow. They see newness as something not yet mastered, rather than something to be avoided. They are more likely to embrace complexity rather than move away from it.

Earlier I talked about improvisation comedy and how important a growth mindset is to making progress. There are a few reasons for this. Improv is about embracing the unknown, having no fear, putting yourself out there, showing vulnerability and learning from the experience. In fact, one of the main reasons why people don't pass the semester is that they are unable to embrace the fear. Improv encourages you to learn by participating in jam sessions (where anyone can get up and join experienced improvisers in front of a live audience). Immersing yourself in this type of experience sets you up to fail and look a little incompetent, but at the same time it opens you up to enormous learning and growth.

One of the reasons why I chose to take improv comedy classes is that it was a way to get out of my comfort zone, feel incompetent, and apply a growth or learning mindset in order to make progress. If I was to adopt a fixed mindset, I would play it safe or, even worse, come to the premature conclusion that my lack of immediate skill meant that this was not for me. However, adopting a growth mindset allowed me to embrace the challenge, adapt and grow.

Ideas for developing a growth mindset

Focus on improving rather than proving your performance

What hinders people with a fixed mindset is that they see challenges and setbacks as reason to avoid a task. Those with a growth mindset focus on the improvements they are making and understand that, when they try something challenging, they will be clunky and awkward at first. They also know that this awkwardness is an important part of the learning process. So, don't get hung up on your performance – just notice the improvement you are making.

I recently attended a yoga retreat in Thailand. I had never done yoga in my life, and I felt inadequate and incompetent. What I focused on was the improvement I made over the two weeks. Initially I didn't see much of an improvement, but by the end of the second week I did. I have continued my yoga practice (twice a week), with slow but steady improvements!

Don't compare yourself to others

This is important. One of the things I notice with individuals who hold a fixed mindset is that they frequently compare themselves to others and end up feeling defeated before they even start. Don't make comparisons! If you are going to compare, then compare your current level of skill to a previous version of yourself. Are you improving? If not, what could you be doing differently? Those with a growth mindset focus on their individual improvements and are motivated by making progress. You may not ever be able to present like the motivational speaker Tony Robbins, but with hard work and enthusiasm, who knows where you can get to with your presentation skills? By all means, learn from others, but set your *own* incremental goals to develop your desired skill.

Be curious about the reasons why you might be struggling to make progress

Those with a fixed mindset see struggling as a lack of innate talent, or a sign that they are unlikely to be good at something. Rather than be curious, they go into avoidance. Those with a growth mindset are more likely to be curious about their struggles and setbacks. They look for the learning, seek out the views of others, ask questions and continue to experiment. If you are tackling something challenging, or you're outside your comfort zone, then it's highly likely that at times things won't go your way. If that's the case, simply explore the reasons why and look for ways to mitigate them.

Ask yourself 'growth mindset' questions

Whenever you undertake a challenging task, want to avoid something or think you will never be good enough, then ask yourself growth mindset questions. These might include:

- What can I learn from this challenge?
- What could I try differently?
- Have I done everything possible to get the best outcome?
- Who else can I learn from?
- How can I see this as an opportunity rather than a challenge?

These questions help shift your perspective to one of learning.

CHAPTER 5

Understand Your Context

Have you ever noticed a particular problem, issue or challenge that keeps coming up? You put in place solutions, but the challenge just won't go away. It might be an issue of low or flagging employee engagement, your team resisting change, poor product quality or changing customer expectations.

One of the main reasons why people don't make progress on these challenges is that they don't spend enough time understanding their context. Many of us have a bias for action: we operate from a sense of urgency – we like to get things done, tick things off the list and move on to the next pressing issue. This works well for some challenges, but it doesn't work for others.

In understanding context, I refer to the excellent work of Ron Heifetz and Marty Linsky from Harvard, two principal thought leaders in the area of Adaptive Leadership.[8] They assert that there are two types of challenges that any system faces: Technical and Adaptive.

Technical challenges are those that operate in a more predictable world, where existing know-how and expertise can solve the issue. There is usually an understood cause and effect for technical challenges. Whilst these issues might be complicated, there is capacity and capability to solve them. For example, a widescale

ATM system outage for one of my large banking clients may require a complicated fix, but there is likely to be an identifiable cause and existing expertise within the bank to resolve the outage.

Adaptive challenges operate more in the unpredictable realm. There is less understanding of cause and effect. There are multiple stakeholders with different opinions, assumptions and values to take into consideration, and what may have worked in the past may not work now. There is a messiness about adaptive challenges. There is far more unpredictability, we can't rely on what's worked in the past, and patterns often unfold in conflict. In these situations, it is less about solving issues and more about making progress. Making progress involves experimenting, learning and experimenting again.

An organisation that is attempting to embed a 'customer-first' culture may think that training frontline staff in delighting the customer is the answer. This may be a technical fix to what is likely to be an adaptive challenge. If we were to treat it as an adaptive challenge, we might find that a better solution would be to reduce responsibilities for the frontline staff, freeing them up to spend time with customers without fear of repercussions if their transactional work is not completed. Implementing this solution will not be easy for either group – hence why this is considered an adaptive challenge – as it requires experimentation, stakeholder engagement, behavioural change at multiple levels and other systemic changes.

There are also those challenges that have both technical and adaptive components. The key in these cases is to spend time understanding your current reality so that you can identify the technical and adaptive components. If you are unable to distinguish between challenges that are technical or complicated and those that are adaptive or complex, then your ability to adapt is diluted, and your natural bias for action may result in the same challenges coming up again and again.

Ideas for understanding your context

Run 'safe to fail' parallel experiments

Dave Snowden, an expert in decision making and complexity, suggests that a way to better understand the context you are operating in is to run a number of 'safe to fail' experiments. He suggests three questions to ask as you frame these experiments[9]:

- What can I change?
- Where can I monitor the impact of that change?
- Where can I rapidly amplify success or dilute/ dampen failure?

The key to these experiments is to run them at the same time and make sure they are 'safe to fail'. You should be able to learn about your context from the experiments and recover from them if they are failing.

Ask, 'What makes this messy?'

When helping clients who are trying to make progress with a change that is important to them, I like to ask the question, 'What makes this messy?' The purpose of this question is to get them away from superficially diagnosing context and forcing them to delve deeper. By resisting the urge to tie things up neatly with a bow, we can begin to truly untangle the issues at the heart of the challenge. These may include multiple stakeholders with competing needs, employees or colleagues who are resistant to change, or our own unconscious biases or assumptions. If you want to understand context, then always ask yourself the question: What makes this messy?

Be a 'systems thinker'

If you want to better understand your situation, we encourage you to practice 'systems thinking'. This practice is about seeing the interrelationship between things, rather than viewing them as separate or simply correlated. Organisations are complex social systems, and one of the mistakes leaders make is ignoring the complexity of the system. It's important to view context as a whole rather than part of a whole. For more on how to become a systems thinker, see Chapter 7.

Try reframing

Reframing a challenge or situation is a good way to better understand the problem or reality you face. It also allows you to avoid inadvertently applying a technical fix to an adaptive challenge. In Thomas Wedell-Wedellsborg's 2017 *Harvard Business Review* article, 'Are You Solving the Right Problems?'[10], he uses the example of people in an office block complaining about a slow lift. The obvious solution is to replace the lift or find a way to quicken the lift. However, if we reframe the problem from 'the lift is too slow' to 'the wait is annoying', we may find that the best solution may not be a quicker lift but might be simply making the wait *feel* shorter. This might involve playing music, installing a hand sanitiser or installing mirrors. The reframing of a problem helps us to see the solution in a different light. One way to reframe a challenge or problem is to get key stakeholders to independently document on stickies or flip charts what they think the problem or challenge is. Too often we mistakenly think we agree on what the challenge is, but documenting can identify differences, help us to reframe the situation, and encourage greater clarity.

CHAPTER 6

Make Conflictual Interpretations of Your Context

A key element of understanding your context is observing and interpreting your current reality before embarking on an appropriate solution. How can we look at a situation through every possible lens rather than take a singular view? Are we more comfortable with taking a safe and benign view of our current reality, or are we prepared to make challenging or conflictual interpretations that help us get to a better understanding of our situation?[11]

Before we explain the role of conflictual interpretations, it is important to remind ourselves of the distinction between observation and interpretation.

Observation is the act of noticing the details and patterns around and within you. It involves collecting data. Imagine capturing what you are seeing with a video camera with no judgement or bias. It is simply being as objective as possible about what you are seeing.

Interpretation is more challenging. People can observe the same event, the same data, and interpret it differently. For example, one person can view someone being marginalised in a meeting and another can interpret it as the person not asserting themselves. The key is to bring these different interpretations to the surface. One interpretation alone constitutes an opinion; many interpretations together create a better representation of reality. Ultimately, this means more options and better solutions.

Multiple interpretations aren't much good to us, however, if they are benign. To truly understand current reality, we need to make conflictual or challenging interpretations. If we stick to the benign or safe interpretation, we may employ a technical or simple fix to an adaptive or complex challenge. It is easy to make safe and benign interpretations that never challenge the status quo, but making conflictual or challenging interpretations helps us get to the heart of our context and making meaningful change. It is easy to blame an umpire for losing a game, but a conflictual interpretation might be that we didn't trust each other on the field or we focused on our own brilliance rather than on our team roles.

Let's use an example. Imagine I get the evaluations back from a two-day intensive workshop I had just run with a colleague. The feedback was not positive. We also observed during the two days that people were disengaged, on their phones, distracted, defensive and not actively participating in the activities. One interpretation could be that the participants didn't get it. Another might be that they were the wrong people on the program. Either of these interpretations may be true, but they may not be. They are benign because they are safe interpretations. Safe in that the interpretations are about the participants and not how we as facilitators might have contributed.

What might be some conflictual or tough interpretations we could make? One conflictual interpretation might be that we as facilitators weren't prepared, or that we didn't work together as a team. It might be that we didn't educate the client upfront on the nature of the program, we made assumptions about the group's readiness, or we didn't trust each other as facilitators.

These interpretations force us to self-reflect and challenge us to own our solutions. It stops us from blaming others and helps us own what we might be contributing.

It is also important to be wary of *default* interpretations that we make. These interpretations are the same ones we come up with time and time again, regardless of the context. They are also examples of benign or safe interpretations. Let me illustrate through an example.

In one leadership team I worked with there was a tendency for the group to blame the organisational culture for their own lack of progress. They believed their busyness, reactiveness and task-focus was simply a result of getting caught up in an organisational culture that demanded that type of behaviour. This cultural dynamic, they felt, was impacting their ability to become a high-performing team. I observed that there was a pattern emerging in the group. When they experienced a lack of progress, their tendency was to blame the organisational culture. I was able to share my observation of this default interpretation and asked them to make some conflictual interpretations. I started by posing the question to the team: 'What are some conflictual interpretations of why this group is not progressing?' In a short time, they were able to come up with: we value our own work over the work of the team; working on this team isn't a priority; we are addicted to the busyness; we are less comfortable in the relational side of our work; and we don't feel safe in this team. These conflictual interpretations helped the team to make a breakthrough in understanding the reality of their failings. It's worth noting that the team's initial interpretation about organisational culture may indeed be valid, but it's important to resist settling on the easiest explanations and to explore other possible interpretations – even if they are uncomfortable or challenging.

Making conflictual interpretations enables us to respond to situations in a more nuanced way. It helps leaders get to the heart of what's going on in an environment that is complex and ambiguous. It also allows us to think differently, rather than see our reality through a preferred worldview.

Ideas for making conflictual interpretations

Identify your part of the 'mess'

One of the best ways to make a conflictual interpretation is to identify your part of the mess. When we make a safe interpretation, we can make it about our stakeholders, our team, our manager, our customers, the industry or market conditions. It is also important to make it about us. In my coaching, I often ask the individual how they might be contributing to the situation. If the team is disengaged, ask yourself how you could be contributing to the situation. If you are in a leadership team grappling with low employee engagement, ask yourself, 'How are we, as a team, contributing to this situation or the "mess"?'

Challenge the default or status quo interpretation

When we are faced with the same issues or challenges popping up, we can often revert to a default or a status quo interpretation. Default interpretations are benign or safe and may not get to the heart of what is going on. Not only is it easy to identify a single interpretation (remember, one interpretation alone is an opinion), it's also easy to go back to that same interpretation again and again. If you want to make conflictual interpretations that lead to real results, then challenge yourself and others about the default interpretations you might be making. One way of doing this is asking people outside of your context or situation to be provocative about what they are seeing. Another way is to get up on the balcony (see Chapter 3) and name the default interpretation, then come back to the dancefloor and challenge people's thinking about why they are landing on the same default interpretation each time.

Ask challenging questions

One way to provide conflictual interpretations is to ask challenging questions. A challenging question put forward with the right intent can encourage others to see things from a different perspective. Challenging questions might include:

- What's our part out the mess? (see previous page)
- If our customers/peers/key stakeholders/ managers/direct reports were in the room, what would they say our issue is?
- What is the loss associated with this issue?
- What are we most fearful of in regard to this issue?
- What elephant in the room are we not surfacing?

CHAPTER 7

Become a Systems Thinker

In the previous chapter we talked about understanding context. If we don't understand context, we can end up applying the wrong solution to complex challenges. When faced with complex challenges, we need to move from conventional and linear thinking towards systems (or systemic) thinking.

What's the difference between conventional thinking and systems thinking?

Conventional thinking is how we might approach a technical challenge (outlined in Chapter 5). Conventional thinking takes a linear approach to responding to challenges where the problem and solution are easily defined. In most cases, cause and effect are known. Conventional thinking focuses on breaking the challenge into parts and working on them in a straightforward; step-by-step way. In this approach, fixing the parts results in fixing the problem. For example, if I break my arm, there is a clear solution: I seek out a doctor to mend the broken arm. The doctor makes an assessment and then performs surgery or puts a cast around the broken arm. They provide instructions on how to manage the healing, and in time the cast comes off. It is a simple, step-by-step procedure.

Systems thinking is more holistic and seeks to understand the challenge as a group of interacting, interrelated and interdependent components that form a complex and unified whole. A system can be an organisation, a division within an organisation, the sector you work in, your family or your relationship. We often hear the terms 'political system' or 'health system' or 'justice system'; these are highly complex, adaptive structures that have many moving parts.

Let's look at an example of the organisation as a system of various interconnections and interrelationships. An organisational system contains the history of the organisation, the current leadership, structure and hierarchy, the culture, sub-cultures, processes, norms, organisational politics, departments, and employees – just to name a few. In the broader organisational system you have suppliers, customers, competitors, the regulatory environment and even the political environment. When making decisions and implementing change, organisations have to think about all of their components. For example, in the health system you have hospitals, patients, governments, pharmaceutical companies, the TGA, alternative health providers, doctors, surgeons, nurses, researchers, media etc. Each of them may have their own needs and agendas. This creates enormous complexity.

When an organisation is facing complex challenges where there are no obvious solutions, it is important to look systemically to see the patterns, themes, connections and interrelationships. The purpose of systems thinking is to widen the lens and to look at issues, problems and challenges more broadly. If we don't understand the broader system, we may end up solving one issue but experiencing an unintended consequence in another part of the system.

Let's use a simple example to explain. Say in your organisation, revenue is decreasing. Conventional thinking might be that you need to find a way to sell more to your existing clients and expand your client base. You go on your merry way of implementing a new account management structure, engaging a sales training company to train staff, and provide monetary incentives for exceeding sales targets. However, rather than increasing sales, you notice in 12 months' time that revenue has decreased again. The logical assumption might be that the sales training didn't work. However, what if you applied a systems lens and looked at what the trends, patterns and themes are across the broader system? You might see that revenue is decreasing in the overall sector due to new alternatives for people to spend their money on, or you might find that there are low-cost competitors coming in, or that the recruitment of sales staff has not resulted in the right people being hired. It might be a number of these issues, or a range of others, and unless you widen your lens and look systemically, you may default to the most obvious solution but not resolve anything. This may also result in financial and human resources being wasted.

Being a systems thinker is an important part of leadership agility. If we don't apply a systemic lens to any system we are part of, we will struggle to operate effectively within that system.

Ideas for becoming a systems thinker

Provide conflictual interpretations

In the previous chapter, I talked about the importance of conflictual interpretations. If you want to apply a system lens to what might be happening in your current reality, then you need to be tough and challenging in your assessment. If we use our revenue example from page 46, we might say a safe interpretation is that our sales people need to sell more. A conflictual or tough interpretation might be that our after-sales service is poor and is resulting in brand damage and losing customers. Don't play with safe interpretations when looking at the system.

Ask 'The Five Whys'

This concept was shown to me many years ago and is also spoken about in Peter Senge's *The Fifth Discipline Fieldbook*[12]. 'The Five Whys' is an iterative questioning technique that is used to highlight cause-and-effect relationships of a problem. The process involves the repeated asking of the question 'why', where each answer determines the next 'why' question. It works well when trying to discover a single root cause. Let's look at an example.

Question	*'Why are we losing revenue?'*
Answer	*'We aren't selling enough.'*
Question	*'Why aren't we selling enough?'*
Answer	*'Our sales people don't have the willingness or skills to sell more.'*
Question	*'Why don't our sales people have the willingness or skills to sell more?'*
Answer	*'We haven't recruited the right people.'*
Question	*'Why haven't we recruited the right people?'*
Answer	*'We haven't modernised our remuneration and incentive packages to keep up with the market and this has hindered our ability to attract good people.'*
Question	*'Why haven't we modernised our remuneration and incentive packages to keep up with the market?'*
Answer	*'It hasn't been an issue until now.'*

The Five Whys help us look at some of the systemic issues that might be impacting on our current reality.

Visualise connections within the system

There are many connections within a system. Systems thinking involves making these connections and seeing an issue with a wide lens. One of the challenges is that systems and patterns are hard to see. We need to visualise them, and one of the ways to do that is to use a white board or flip chart paper and map the system. Where are things connected? This also gets everyone to see what is in the system. If we think about our sales example, using this technique we might find a connection between lower employee engagement and poor after-sales service. By visualising connections and widening our lens, we can find a better or more appropriate solution to our problem.

Get comfortable with using hypotheses

When viewing a system, use a hypothesis to test what you are seeing. A hypothesis is a guess or a theory based on what you are observing. It is temporary and is constantly being updated as new facts come to light. You can even use your journal to do this. Write down your hypothesis and continually refine what you're seeing. Each hypothesis should be shared, challenged, tested and examined for a new and better hypothesis. In systems thinking we are trying to guess at the truth and get closer to it. Continually updating your hypothesis will help you achieve this.

CHAPTER 8

Embrace Dualities

Kathy Mattea, a Grammy award-winning artist, once said, 'That's the great paradox of living on this earth, that in the midst of great pain you can have great joy as well. If we didn't have those things we'd just be numb.' In our professional and personal world, paradoxes or dualities are everywhere, and rather than try to resolve them we need to manage them.

A duality is something that has seemingly contradictory elements or qualities. We see dualities at a societal level. For example, how do we encourage aspiration and at the same time have a safety net for those less fortunate? How do we reduce our carbon emissions using alternative energy sources and at the same time keep energy costs down, and power supply secure and stable? In our day-to-day work, it might be delivering results at the same time as building relationships, or delivering short-term results and building capability for the future.

In our own personal lives we see these dualities at play. Work–life balance provides a classic example of a duality, where you want to meet the expectations of your manager and your team, and at the same time meet the expectations of your partner and children. In my own life I experience the duality of wanting to run long distances, and knowing I need to rest and re-energise.

This is actually difficult for me as I can see strongly the advantages of one (the running,) but less so the other (the resting). With an injury in the lead-up to the 2018 Berlin Marathon I learnt the powerful lesson of not managing this duality with a strong focus on my running and not on my resting. I should be practicing what I preach more often!

With dualities there is a natural tension, and we often treat them either consciously or unconsciously as an 'either/or' problem to solve when in fact the conflicting needs or wants need to be managed at the same time. In other words, how do we manage the upside of both rather than focus on one over the other?

One of my coaching clients, Karen, had some feedback that her strong focus on outcomes was coming at a cost to her relationships and engagement with her team. She tended to micromanage to ensure she got the outcomes she was looking for. When we started the coaching process, Karen was worried that if she focused more on relationships it would impact negatively on the results she was looking to deliver.

This is classic 'either/or' thinking, or what Jim Collins, the author of *Built to Last*[13], highlighted as the 'Tyranny of the OR'. I encouraged Karen to start looking at outcomes and engagement with her team as a 'both/and' situation. In other words, what could she do to build relationships and engagement with her team AND deliver the outcomes she wanted?

Barry Johnson, a thought leader in polarity thinking (dualities[14]), has developed a framework which I used to help Karen. The focus of the framework is identifying the following:

▶ The benefits of focusing on one element of the duality (e.g. delivering tasks/outputs).

▶ The downsides of focusing on this element and avoiding the competing element.

▶ The positive results from focusing on the other element of the duality (e.g. building long-term capability).

▶ The downsides of focusing on this element and avoiding the competing element.

▶ A set of actions that ensure we have upside on each of the competing elements.

The results of the activity that I used with Karen are in the table below:

MANAGING DUALITY EXAMPLE		
	Delivery of Task	Building Long-term Capability of Team
STEP 1	What are the benefits?	What are the benefits?
	• Meets defined goals • Meets expectation of line manager • Helps meet stakeholder/customer expectations • Personally satisfied • Increased quality • Timely	• Increased diversity of ideas • Team takes ownership of team goals • Deeper engagement and satisfaction of team • Higher motivation • Increased trust • Increased ability to influence • Takes pressure off the individual to deliver

cont. next page

	Delivery of Task	Building Long-term Capability of Team
STEP 2	**What are the downsides of focusing on this side and avoiding the other?**	**What are the downsides of focusing on this side and avoiding the other?**
	• Low morale and engagement • Long hours • Burnout/Stress/Health Issues • Isolation • Seen as autocratic • Builds bad habits • May not get promoted past this level	• Tasks not being delivered • Short-term quality issues • Potential for deadlines to be missed • Feeling less valued • Less control
STEP 3	**What do I need to do (actions) to ensure we have positive results in this area?**	**What do I need to do (actions) to ensure we have positive results in this area?**
	• Keep a project that I want to work on • Manage stakeholder and manager expectations moving forward • Implement a delegation plan to the team • Introduce team members to key stakeholders	• Hold one-on-one meetings to identify development needs and strengths • Craft development plans for each team member • Implement delegation plan • Create feedback loops around the allocation of tasks • Share vulnerability around letting go of the work

Over several months, Karen implemented the above actions and started to lift the capability of her team, delegated more and managed stakeholder expectations. This resulted in improved stakeholder and employee relationships.

Through awareness of the dualities we experience, we are able to develop actions that encourage less 'either/or' thinking and more 'both/and' thinking. This enables us to better manage the dualities we face every day in organisations and in life.

Ideas for embracing dualities

Identify a personal duality that you grapple with

One way of doing this is to think about some of the strengths you overuse (see Chapter 26) and those you underuse. Do you like change and ambiguity or prefer control and stability? Do you find you're good with people but struggle to have difficult conversations around accountability? You may have a duality that has innovation on one side and compliance on the other. Both are equally important, but with a strong focus on innovation, you may be neglecting the importance of compliance. Chat to a coach or someone who knows you well to work out what your strengths are and what you neglect as a result. This will provide clarity on a duality you could more effectively manage.

Move to 'both/and' thinking

Once you have identified your duality, I encourage
you to move from an 'either/or' style of thinking to a
'both/and' style of thinking. For example, notice when
you are preferencing something over something else,
or notice when you are engaging in black-and-white
thinking. Use the table on page 53–54 to help better
understand the impact of your duality and how you can
use strategies to manage them. The key is to see the
advantages and disadvantages of both, and to embrace
the 'and'.

Manage your duality

I encourage you to manage your duality by
implementing action steps or small experiments
(see Chapter 23) that enhance both sides. Refer to the
earlier table for examples of some action steps or small
experiments. The key is to experiment with behaviours
and actions that get the balance right. If one of your
elements is outcome-focused (which is your stronger
preference), and the other is relationship focused, then
I would encourage you to implement small actions and
experiments that enhance your relationship focus.

CHAPTER 9

Demonstrate Curiosity

Curiosity is so important, whether it be in developing a growth mindset (Chapter 4), embracing a different perspective (Chapter 17), showing empathy (Chapter 16) or understanding your stakeholders' world (Chapter 21).

Without curiosity, it's hard to imagine creative ideas and innovation taking place. Curiosity helps us stay open to uncertainty and complexity, and it encourages us to engage with others in a way that reduces conflict and brings people together. Francesca Gino, in her 2018 *Harvard Business Review* article 'The Business Case for Curiosity'[15] highlighted that curiosity in the workplace has a number of benefits. These include fewer decision-making errors (we are more aware of cognitive biases impacting our decisions), more innovation and creativity, reduced group conflict, more open communication, and better team performance.

Unfortunately, I don't see as much curiosity as I would like in the work I do with my clients. There are a number of reasons for this, including a task-focused mindset, busyness and a bias for action, a desire to stay true to your world view, and perfectionism (needing to get everything right). Curiosity requires us to ask questions, assume we don't have all the answers, and view life as an opportunity to learn, experiment more and diversify our interests.

To me, it is about developing a childlike wonder in the way we see the world.

One of the first books I read after starting my consulting practice was *Geeks and Geezers* by Warren G Bennis and Robert J Thomas[16]. If you haven't read this book, I would highly recommend doing so. It looks at the values, qualities and moments that defined a group of older leaders (geezers) and younger leaders (geeks) who were outstanding in their fields. There were two concepts that stood out for me when reading this book:

▶ The first is that both groups shared adaptive capacity (similar to agility).
▶ The second is the concept of 'neoteny', and the role it played with geezers in improving their ability to adapt and continuously learn.

Neoteny is a zoological term that means the retention of juvenile qualities in the adult animal. Bennis and Thomas explain it in the context of these geezers as 'the retention of all those wonderful qualities that we associate with youth: curiosity, playfulness, eagerness, fearlessness, warmth, energy'[17]. The authors noted that the success of the geezers was due to many of these qualities, which are synonymous with learning and leadership agility.

In my workshops I often ask participants, 'Which demographic in our society is the most curious and best learners?' The response is always 'children', and the reasons given include their innate inquisitiveness and willingness to ask lots of questions, their lack of fear, their vulnerability and openness around learning, their readiness to experiment, and their constant thirst for knowledge.

If you have children, or nieces and nephews, you will see this curiosity and learning at its purest. We come into the world full of natural curiosity and interest in how things work. We constantly ask questions, we experiment, we play, we explore and we show a desire to learn. We don't see problems; we see puzzles to be solved. We use our imaginations to spark ideas rather than focus on why things can't be done. When children discover things, it gives them pleasure and a desire to discover more. This constant focus on discovery leads to mastery. If you have children in your life that know more than you about dinosaurs or frogs or the solar system, you will know what I am talking about.

Over the years I have loved watching my nieces when they are in a playful mode. I particularly enjoy noticing their language. They never say, 'That won't work,' or 'That's a dumb idea,' or 'We tried something similar in the past and it failed' (sound familiar?). There is never that 'not invented here' syndrome that you often hear about in organisations. (The 'not invented here' syndrome is where people resist new ideas and changes because they didn't come up with them. Therefore, their view is that they won't work.) Instead, my nieces say things like, 'Why don't we try this?' or 'Wow, that was fun,' or they simply laugh as they try some novel idea regardless of whether it works or not. It is infectious!

Another factor that accelerates the learning of children is immediate feedback. We don't wait six months for their annual performance review to give them the feedback that riding their bike in the dark without lights is not a good thing to do. We give them the feedback there and then. Sure, children make mistakes, but we generally encourage learning from these mistakes rather than punishing them. The key to killing learning and curiosity is a lot of 'don't' statements and fear. The more we punish, provoke fear and constantly tell children, 'Don't do this, don't do that,' we limit their ability to learn and grow. It is the same for adults.

This natural curiosity that we were born with can wane over time as we start to enjoy routine, certainty and familiarity. The qualities that make children great learners can also be discouraged in us as we grow older. We become rule followers, we start aiming to please people, and we struggle to show vulnerability because we want to look smart and competent. We develop biases, we make assumptions, we seek to judge, and we place emphasis on efficiency to the detriment at times of learning and a quality outcome.

Curiosity, or expressing a sense of childlike wonder, is such a vital component of leadership agility. It helps us to stay open to possibilities, to look at problems from multiple perspectives, and helps to spark our imagination and, in turn, our ideas. It also helps us find different ways to engage with people who have a different view to us.

Ideas for developing your curiosity

Get out and play

In their book *Play*[18], Stuart Brown and Christopher Vaughan discuss the importance of play, and how it shapes our imaginations and helps us to be more resilient and adaptable. For adults, play can take many forms, including getting out in nature, spending time with playful people such as children, attending theatre and improvisation classes, cooking without a recipe, completing jigsaw puzzles, solving puzzle rooms, writing a creative story and exploring your city as though you are a tourist. Look for any experiences that might expose you to novelty. The list is endless. Just remember, the most important thing is that you approach the activity in a playful mode and not as a chore.

I am currently in Bali as I write this. I am on a co-working retreat and exposing myself to a range of playful things including yoga, meditation, ecstatic dance, chanting and Cacao ceremonies. I am noticing the joy and fun of doing things I wouldn't normally do. It allows me to stay open rather than closed.

Become a 'curious scientist'

I often run a mindfulness exercise where I ask people to look at a dried apricot as though they are a curious scientist who hasn't seen such an object before. Some of the questions I ask are: What do you notice? What looks unusual? What hadn't you seen before that you see now? It always proves to be an eye-opening task. Try this at home with something from your fruit bowl or fridge. Sit down with a notepad and tap into the mind of a curious scientist. Write down your answers to these questions, and anything else unusual that you may notice. In fact do, it with any day-to-day object that you use and see what you notice. The key is to notice novelty.

Ask questions

If you want to develop curiosity, don't be afraid to ask questions. Asking more questions helps us to understand the world around us. Many people are unwilling to ask questions when they don't understand something, as they fear it may make them look foolish in front of others. Sometimes asking questions does require vulnerability, but, if you're not sure of something, it's always best to simply ask. Learn to ask the right questions that help you and others to better understand a problem. Those questions should be open-ended and start with a 'how', 'why', 'what' or 'when'. You might like to ask the same question, but each time encourage a different response. By the third time you might notice novelty in the response emerging. Stay away from questions that are closed and generate a yes or no response. To complement asking questions, listen deeply to answers. In my experience, curious people are very good listeners, and they let go of ego as they listen. We discuss this more in Chapter 14.

CHAPTER 10

Practice Mindfulness

You may have heard about mindfulness through the media, or even practiced it during a workshop or seminar that you attended. The practice of mindfulness is growing rapidly in organisations, not just as a great way to manage stress and regulate emotions, but also as a way to help individuals make behavioural change. In a world that is fast-paced and changing, mindfulness enables us to respond to situations more effectively whilst simultaneously advancing our wellbeing in the workplace. Without being mindful we operate on autopilot, and often miss novelty and nuance in the world around us.

So, what is mindfulness? I define mindfulness as 'the practice of bringing attention to your present experience without judgement in a formal or informal way'.

There are several components to this definition that I want to highlight. The first is being 'present'. Mindfulness is about the here and now, bringing attention to what is happening in the moment. It might be a conversation you are having with someone, thinking about a tricky staff issue, walking along the beach or drinking a glass of wine. Whatever you are doing, it is about staying in the present and being aware of what is happening in the moment.

The second component is 'without judgement'. One of the essential elements of mindfulness is observing your thoughts and feelings without judgement. We are constantly in our heads thinking, and we can get caught up in or hijacked by our thoughts every day.

What mindfulness teaches is to observe your thoughts with openness and curiosity. Don't judge yourself by the type and frequency of your thoughts, just notice them.

Mindfulness can also be formal or informal. Formal mindfulness usually occurs through mindfulness meditation. Mindfulness meditation involves creating formal space in your day to practice being present without judgement. One of the simplest and most popular ways of doing this is through breathing. We choose breathing because it grounds us in the here and now. Simply focus on your breath, both the inhale and exhale. For me, I like to practice mindfulness when I run. I use it as an opportunity to be in the here and now by focusing on my breath. I rarely think about anything but my breathing and my running step. I do this particularly on my longer weekly runs (90+ mins), and it helps keep me grounded. You could also try yoga as the focus is on staying present by breathing into your postures (asanas). Most mindful meditation uses the breath to help stay in the moment.

Mindfulness can also happen informally. Informal mindfulness is the opposite of multitasking. It is about being present to the single task you are involved in. It is having a conversation with a team member without being distracted by something else. It is being in a meeting without being on your iPad. Informal mindfulness can be very useful when making behavioural change. When I am coaching individuals who want to make behavioural change, I ask them to develop awareness of the behaviour they want to change in real time. I encourage them to become mindful of that behaviour and of the different choice they want to make.

They don't have to always get it right (remember, I don't want them to judge), but I want them to be aware, because without awareness they have no ability to make the change. Mindfulness gets them off autopilot.

One of my clients, Jess, is what I would call a strong leader. She is bright, confident and very outcome-focused. She received feedback as part of our coaching process that at times she could be directive rather than facilitative in her team meetings. Her directive behaviours involved making most of the decisions, dominating the conversation, advising the team, answering most of the questions and showing impatience when the things got bogged down. As Jess was action-oriented, she wanted solutions straight away as to how she could be more facilitative or show more of a coaching style. I took a different tack and asked her to slow down, be present and mindful in her team meetings, and just observe and notice what she does. Jess documented her observations over a number of interactions with team members and she was blown away by how many times she fell into a directive style. We then worked together on staying mindful and present, whilst introducing some different behaviours, particularly around asking questions and listening. This proved remarkably helpful to Jess and her team.

There are many benefits to mindfulness. It was originally developed to tackle stress and anxiety, encouraging people to let go of their thoughts rather than judge and ruminate on them. Mindfulness may not change the experiences we have, but it can change the way we view them. As mentioned above, it can help us make behavioural change by bringing awareness to our behaviour and its consequences. Mindfulness reduces anxiety, increases concentration and alertness, and supports overall wellbeing. This is particularly important when leading in complex times.

Mindfulness also increases the quality of your work. I run a one-day workshop that I have been doing for some time now. It is easy to go on autopilot when you have done something a number of times, but I am really conscious of staying mindful as if it is the first time I have presented the material. I use a mantra before I start, which is: 'This is the first time I have presented to this group.' I also look over my slides before the session starts just to get me in the present. I am usually more satisfied, and the evaluations are testament to that as well.

Leadership agility requires mindful practice. Every day the pace and the complexity of change encourages us to take short cuts, to multitask and essentially be mindless. Mindfulness helps us step back from the busyness and gain perspective. If we are being mindless then it impairs our ability to be nimble and adaptable.

Ideas for practicing mindfulness

Start small

The first step to practicing mindfulness is to get started. There are a variety of ways to do this. It might be going for a walk and bringing attention to the colours you observe or the sounds you hear. You might mindfully drink a glass of wine, and savour the aroma and flavour. You could mindfully eat your lunch, paying close attention to the various tastes and textures. You might sit in a quiet space and focus on your breathing for five minutes a day.

The key is to make a start, no matter how small.

Don't get frustrated

When you start mindfulness practice, you may notice yourself feeling distracted by other thoughts and find it challenging. This is normal. Just notice those distracting thoughts and imagine they are on a leaf floating down a river. Let them go without judgement. This is the beauty of mindfulness. We are never perfect from the get-go, so don't get frustrated. Frustration can be a natural emotion we experience when doing something new. Like anything worth doing, it takes practice.

Stop multitasking

We all multitask, thinking we are being more efficient, but there is enough evidence to suggest that multitasking adds to our stress and reduces the quality of the tasks we are trying to complete. We have become so addicted to multitasking that some of us even text and drive, which impairs our driving in the same way alcohol does. We walk the streets on our phones without noticing things around us, such as a red light. We mindlessly watch TV and surf our iPad simultaneously, not fully engaging with either activity. Multitasking stops us from being present and in the moment. Multitasking is about doing, and mindfulness is about being. If you want to become more mindful, then avoid multitasking wherever possible.

Use all the help you can get

There are so many resources out there to help you practice mindfulness. Just google mindfulness resources and there are guided meditations, exercises and workshops. I use an app called Insight Timer which gives me access to 15,000 free meditations. You can use a silent or a guided meditation, depending on your mood. I started meditation as a daily practice in early 2019. Up until then I was sporadic. In three months I can already see the difference in my ability to stay present.

Chapter 11

Manage Your Cognitive Biases

I want to challenge some of the clichés around trusting your gut. Are you one of those individuals who are prone to making quick decisions, relying on a gut feeling or intuition? Whether it be appraising a person when you first meet them or making a recruitment choice based on how similar they are to you; many of your 'gut' decisions are subject to biases and assumptions, often resulting in a wrong decision or poor judgement. The impact of these often unknown, implicit biases and assumptions is that they stop us from being curious and open, they impair our judgement and decision making, and they can impact our relationships negatively. They impede our ability to be cognitively agile and to think differently.

To better understand how we are subject to unconscious biases and assumptions, it is important to mention the work of Daniel Kahneman, a Nobel Prize laureate, who is known for his work on judgement, decision making and behavioural economics. In his seminal book titled *Thinking, Fast and Slow*[19], he discusses two 'systems' in the brain: System 1 and System 2.

System 1 is the automatic or instinctual part of the brain

It processes things quickly, automatically, with little or no effort. When you are driving home, this part of the brain switches on and the task is automated, giving you time to think about other things or chat to your passenger. In this case, you can do multiple things at once with ease. System 1 is where our opinions about things are formed very quickly. Many of our daily decisions use this part of the brain. In our working day, we frequently use this system whilst performing regular tasks, such as replying to emails and filing documents. A well-known metaphor would be the 'hare'.

System 2 is the deliberate part of the brain

It is slower, deliberate, reflective, analytical and more subject to reason. It is responsible for more sophisticated functions, such as planning, setting goals, exhibiting self-control and dealing with complex problems. To use a car example again, imagine that you are driving in the United States for the first time in, say, New York City. It would be very difficult to rely on System 1 thinking as the environment and conditions would be completely different to what you are used to. This is where System 2 comes into play, allowing you to concentrate on the differences and take time to adjust to the new situation. You would unlikely want to be chatting to your passenger much, as your energy would be focused on acclimating to the new conditions. In a work situation, you would tap into System 2 thinking when discussing a new product idea or considering a difficult staffing issue. It takes incredible effort and energy to tap into System 2 thinking, and thus our deliberate brain can be a little lazy and overly reliant on System 1. This part of the brain, as a metaphor, would be the 'tortoise'.

Both systems are useful if leveraged properly, but in a fast-paced and complex world, we are prone to over rely on System 1 because we desire both action and simplicity. System 1 is great at simplifying our complex environment. It doesn't like grey areas, ambiguity or complexity. System 1 takes short cuts, makes assumptions, jumps to conclusions and relies on stereotypes to manage the intricacies of the real world. Psychologists call these short cuts 'cognitive biases' or 'heuristics', and there are plenty of them (over 200) that we fall for every day, both in our work and in our personal life. These unconscious biases can have a significant impact on who we recruit and include in our teams, dilute our diversity of thinking, and impede our ability to innovate and create.

There are many cognitive biases that play out in the workplace. The two that I see most regularly are:

1. **Confirmation bias.** This is where our brain seeks out and favours information that confirms our beliefs and assumptions, and ignores information that contradicts them. It is this 'mental model' that helps us process information quickly. We all like to think that we are rational and logical in the way we see things, but studies show that this is not the case. In the workplace, if you assume a particular stakeholder is tricky to deal with, then your brain will seek out data to confirm this assumption. If someone makes a good early impression, we are likely to seek out additional data or arguments that support this belief. If we decide that an idea is a good one, we will look for data to support that rather than open ourselves up to data that may challenge our decision. Conformation bias dilutes leadership agility; it significantly impacts our decision making, as well as our ability to stay open to views that might be different to our own.

2. **Projection bias.** This refers to our tendency to assume that other people see things the same way we do. The average person assumes that their way of thinking about things is typical of most people, and therefore other normal people will come to

the same conclusion as them. For example, I might like to be motivated by praise and recognition, so I assume and project that others feel the same way as I do, when in fact others might like to be motivated in different ways, such as increased responsibility or more challenging work. Our projection bias stops us from staying open and curious; it assumes people are like us and ignores diversity of thinking. It stops us asking questions and narrows our perspectives. This is detrimental to our ability to be agile as leaders.

These are just two examples of the many biases and short cuts our brains make, and I encourage you to read Kahneman's book *Thinking, Fast and Slow* to get a deeper understanding of them.

So, what do cognitive biases mean for leadership agility? Biases stop us from staying open and curious, and impact on learning. They also impact on our ability to deeply understand context. Biases discourage diversity of thinking and embracing different perspectives.

Ideas for managing your cognitive biases

Know and accept that you have unconscious biases

One of the first things is to recognise and accept that your brain takes short cuts that you are usually unaware of. These unconscious biases, assumptions, opinions and beliefs play out every day, and sometimes they get us into trouble. If we can operate from a space knowing that we have these unconscious biases, we are in a better position to notice and challenge them.

Identify your specific cognitive biases

Start noticing when you are making assumptions or rushing to judgement. Where are you judgemental with people? Do you sum people up based on first impressions? Are you prone to stereotyping groups? What strong beliefs do you carry around? What assumptions are you making about this situation? Each of these cognitive biases will stop you from staying open and curious, so pick one that you want to work on and develop a strategy to subvert it.

Practice mindfulness

We discussed the importance of mindfulness in Chapter 10. If we see mindfulness as being present and receptive to what we are experiencing, then this will help us become more aware of our cognitive biases. Mindfulness is another way of getting your System 2 into action. It enables you to be more focused, deliberate and potentially make a better choice.

Test your assumptions and reasoning using the 'Ladder of Inference'

The Ladder of Inference was developed by Harvard Professor Chris Argyris and was later popularised by Peter Senge[20]. The Ladder of Inference describes the thinking pattern we go through, often unconsciously, to get from a fact to a decision or action. We move quickly through this thinking pattern due to our bias for action and quick decisions.

There are generally seven steps in this thinking process:

1. Observe data.
2. Select data from observations.
3. Add meaning to the data from a personal and cultural perspective.
4. Make assumptions based on the meaning added.
5. Draw conclusions based on assumptions made.
6. Adopt beliefs based on these conclusions.
7. Finally, take actions based on those beliefs.

As we move up the Ladder of Inference, we apply biases on the data we see and select, and we apply biases on the meaning and assumptions we make. So how do we stop ourselves from moving unconsciously through this thinking process? The first step is to recognise that we 'select data', make assumptions and draw meaning based on our *own* personal experiences. That doesn't mean you are right or wrong, but it's important to understand that the conclusions you draw will be filtered by your world view. Through greater reflection at each step of the process, you can become more aware of your thinking patterns. The key is to test your assumptions and the meaning or insights you are making. You might do this by documenting or sharing with others your thinking process and the assumptions you are making. Discuss what data supports your ideas. This will enable others to test your thinking and to provide an alternative perspective. We will discuss this more in Chapter 20 on generative dialogue.

Increase your perspectives

Surround yourself with people who think differently to you. One of the things I do when making an important decision or facing a 'people' dilemma is bounce it off my colleague, Janet. What I love about Janet is that she sees things very differently to me. She is relational and empathic, and is very good at walking in the shoes of others. She helps me see things by challenging the assumptions I am making, drawing attention to any biases that might be playing out, or simply offering a different view. I encourage you to find someone who thinks differently to you to test your own thinking processes around important decisions and actions.

ENGAGING DIFFERENTLY

In 2018 I had a coaching assignment with a senior Program Director, Murray. I was asked by Murray's manager to meet with him to see if he would be willing to undertake coaching. The first thing that struck me when I met with Murray was how wedded to his view of the world he was. The feedback from his 360 report and his stakeholders was that he was hardworking and competent but difficult to work with. His manager was particularly strong in his feedback about Murray's inability to constructively engage with others.

I asked Murray about his relationship with his stakeholders, including his manager. Murray explained that he felt that he wasn't being listened to and this frustrated him. He recognised that he wanted to have a better relationship with his manager, but didn't see anything he personally could do differently. Meanwhile, he felt there were many things his manager could do differently. In Murray's mind, everyone else had to change and not him.

If we are to survive and thrive in times of complexity, we must recognise the social and political environment we operate in. We need to appreciate that people are different to us. They may have perspectives, values, beliefs and experiences that create a world view that will be different to ours. In Murray's case he was frustrated because he expected others would see the world in the same way he did. He was unwilling to understand their perspective and to see the world from their vantage point.

Individuals who are effective at engaging differently are deep listeners. They listen to understand and not just for their cue to talk. They show empathy towards others and themselves. They are willing to be vulnerable. They build psychological safety that enables real conversations to be had. They tap into the diverse and sometimes challenging views of others because, for them, diverse and challenging views are what facilitate their learning. In this section I talk about some of the practices that will help you engage differently. This will include: how to build leadership density, how to create psychological safety, how to listen deeply, how to be trustworthy, the importance of embracing different perspectives and productive conflict, and how to engage others with generative dialogue.

CHAPTER 12

Build Leadership Density

One of the classic myths about leadership is that leadership is tied to a hierarchical position. You're a General Manager or a Prime Minister, and therefore that makes you a leader. But your position has nothing to do with leadership. Leadership is about what you do, not about the position you hold.

There are limitations with the concept of the heroic or strong leader, particularly as environments are becoming more and more complex. We think about leaders as charismatic, powerful and influential figures who can lead organisations through challenging times by the sheer force of their personality. Ron Heifetz, who we first met in Chapter 3 as the developer of the 'Balcony and the Dancefloor 'metaphor, is critical of leadership theory that celebrates the normative view of transformational leadership, because it relies too much on the skills of a single person, usually at the top of an organisation.

In an organisational system where there is stability and little complexity, the role of the positional leader or the authority figure is important in establishing and communicating a vision, setting performance objectives, making decisions and delivering outcomes. When the organisation or community or even society is experiencing complexity or facing adaptive challenges, we still look to the position-based leader (such as the CEO or the Prime Minister) to provide the answers. Unfortunately, looking to the position-based leader where adaptive challenges need to be resolved can be problematic. This leads to another myth about leadership where we expect the 'leader' to have the knowledge and expertise to provide all the answers we need to resolve tough problems. When they don't have the answers or meet our expectations, we marginalise them. In organisations, we complain about senior management, and in politics we remove political leaders. As I write this, Australia has had six prime ministers in eight years, and likely seven in nine years soon, based on the latest opinion polls. Hardly a ringing endorsement of the political leadership in this country.

We can't expect leaders to have all the skills and knowledge to solve every challenge, to come up with all the best ideas whilst driving innovation and delivering major change. It is virtually impossible to find someone who can do all of that. In organisations such as Facebook, Amazon, Netflix and Pixar, many of the best ideas and innovation come from those closest to the challenges, and often more junior in the hierarchy. What 'leaders' do well in these organisations is create an environment where everyone can contribute their ideas. Vineet Nayar from the Italian organisation HCL states that[21]:

'Leaders must avoid the urge to answer every question or provide a solution to every problem . . . you must start asking questions, seeing others as the source of [innovation] . . . [this] unleashes the power of the many, thus increasing the speed and quality of innovation and decision making.'

It's rare to meet a CEO or senior leader who by decree can embed innovation in an organisation, eliminate organisational silos and improve employee engagement.

Whenever I talk about complex and adaptive challenges in my workshops and get participants to identify them, I ask whether the CEO, the person with the most authority, could solve these challenges, and the answer is always a resounding 'no'. Why? Because their authority and their position are not enough. This is why we need to think about leadership differently. We can't create a culture of dependence on people who are unable to solve our most complex challenges. We need to create leadership density (where leadership is distributed across the many rather than the few) by tapping into the collective intelligence of communities and organisations, and encourage everyone to exercise leadership. Interestingly, when I ask participants who can solve the big challenges the organisation faces, there is always the same response . . . 'All of us!'

My view of leadership is influenced by Heifetz and Linsky[22], as well as my own work with clients. I think of leadership as a practice that engages others around change that matters. It can be exercised anywhere at any time by anyone, and it can be discrete or sustained.

Let's dissect this view of leadership. First, it defines leadership as a practice or something that you do. You can see it. Leadership is in the action rather than in the title.

Second, it engages others. Leadership is not about self but is about engaging and mobilising others around change that is important, whether that be to the team, the organisation or the community. The day-to-day work of running the business is part of the authority and power that exists within your position.

Third, you can see leadership exercised anywhere across your organisation or community, by anyone at any time. It doesn't matter whether you are an individual in the community, a team member, a local politician, the receptionist, or a Department Head – you have the capacity to exercise leadership.

Finally, it can be discrete or a once off. I think there are times we expect leadership to be present within people all of the time. However, an act of leadership can be discrete. I remember working with a team where one of the quiet members called out an elephant in the room. That immediately changed the conversation from one that was circling to one that became real. That small act of leadership helped the group move forward on a change that was really important to them. However, it can obviously be sustained over a period of time with repeated acts of leadership.

If you want to be more agile, you will need to tap into the ideas, intelligence and advocacy of everyone. This involves building leadership density by sharing power rather than using your position. Imagine a world where everyone is exercising more leadership. It has the power to transform organisations and communities, to make progress on change that is meaningful.

Ideas for building leadership density

Give the work back

One of the concepts that Ron Heifetz, Alexander Grashow and Marty Linsky[23] talk about when building leadership capacity is giving the work back. It is often tempting for 'leaders' to protect their team by keeping the difficult work for themselves. There is a temptation to be strong and to provide clarity and certainty in times of complexity. Giving the work back resists this view and encourages the 'leader' to create an environment where people lean into the complexity and are encouraged to exercise leadership. This is not about delegating, which many people think giving the work back is. Delegating involves distributing tasks and activities. Giving the work back is a way of distributing leadership. Some methods of giving the work back may include: resisting getting involved in work where your team may be looking for your direction; ensuring those closest to the work better understand the system they operate in and the problem/challenge they are facing; encouraging your team to make multiple and tough interpretations of what they are seeing and experiencing; asking lots of questions of your team, rather than providing lots of answers; encouraging experimentation and rewarding those who do exercise leadership.

Create psychological safety

I cover this in the next chapter and it is not my intention to rehash it here, other than to say that if we want those around us to exercise more leadership, then we need to create an environment where people feel free to express relevant thoughts and feelings without judgement or being marginalised. So, show curiosity towards other people's ideas. Delight in their willingness to take an interpersonal risk. It is up to each of us to practice inclusion and encourage everyone to exercise more leadership.

Move beyond the hero paradigm of leadership

Let go of your need to be the 'boss' and the strong leader all of the time. You don't have all the answers and you can't fix all of the problems. If you want to make progress on complex challenges, then you need to involve those around you. Invest time in learning rather than just focusing on outcomes and results. You can't drive change and innovation from the hierarchy, so let go of that need to rescue and be the hero. Your people will thank you for it!

CHAPTER 13

Creating Psychological Safety

In a recent podcast[24] I was listening to, Laszlo Bock, the former Head of People Operations at Google, was speaking about what Google did to create high-performing teams. He evaluated all the Google teams that were considered to be high-performing and distilled their success down to five key elements. First amongst them was the concept of psychological safety. Psychological safety, a concept developed by Harvard Business School Professor Amy Edmondson, describes the 'climate in which people feel free to express relevant thoughts and feelings'.[25] Team members feel safe to take interpersonal risks, and there is confidence that they will not be marginalised or embarrassed for speaking up. There is interpersonal trust and mutual respect in which people are comfortable being themselves. People are encouraged to make mistakes, take risks, experiment and challenge the status quo, offer opinions and engage in productive conflict[26].

I remember working with a senior leadership team a few years back where conversations were polite, benign and frustrating. Some individuals would hold back for fear of saying the wrong thing, and others would take inordinate lengths of time to get their point across in a way that wasn't seen as critical of those around them. It was evident that there was little trust in the group to raise the difficult issues.

The main reason for this was a lack of psychological safety, and this was due to a leader who was deploying his authority in a way that stopped people from speaking up about the real issues. Without psychological safety, it is difficult to demonstrate leadership agility at either an individual or a team level. To lead successfully, we need to be able to debate the real issues, address any elephants in the room, and challenge the status quo without fear of being marginalised.

Whilst a lack of trust can prevent people from speaking up, other reasons include a fear of looking silly in front of colleagues or a fear of being seen as negative. Some people defer to authority as they don't feel safe challenging the more senior people in a room. Whatever the reasons are for not speaking up, it can result in a detrimental impact on the team's progress. It is easy to stay in a comfort zone where we are safe. Why raise concerns if the group's default is to either not deal with them or marginalise someone who does raise them? This can result in 'groupthink', where groups value harmony and conformity so much that it impacts negatively on their decision making.

In her book, *Teaming*[27], Amy Edmondson identified a number of important reasons to foster psychological safety in teams:

- ▶ It encourages people to speak up, to offer conflictual interpretations and address difficult issues.
- ▶ It allows for clarity of issues and challenges. A lack of psychological safety creates anxiety and confusion.
- ▶ People are encouraged to engage in productive conflict or debate issues without fear that there will be personal attacks or passive aggressive behaviour.
- ▶ It encourages experimentation, trial and error, prototyping and learning.

▶ It promotes new ideas.

▶ It increases accountability. People are more willing to put their hand up when mistakes are made, as long as there is a focus on learning.

These reasons create a compelling argument for instilling psychological safety into teams.

So, what are the warning signs that a team might not have psychological safety? The signs I see include people constantly looking to the leader for the answers, conversations that go in a circular motion and never get to the point, people not speaking up, elephants in the room that go unacknowledged, a lack of experimentation or challenging the status quo, criticism of others, people pointing out failures, and people shifting accountability.

One thing to note about psychological safety is that it doesn't require you to be polite or play nice. Psychological safety is about having candid conversations, which may at times feel conflictual. If you want to advance the agility of your team and make progress on issues that matter, then do your best to build psychological safety within your team. When I am working with leadership teams, this is the area that I focus on first.

Ideas for developing psychological safety

Be aware of your own contribution to psychological safety in your team

We all contribute to the psychological safety of a team, whether we lead one or operate as a team member. Are you prone to criticising ideas that are different to your own, ignoring ideas that seem 'out there', marginalising people by interrupting or talking over them, dominating the conversation, or making all the decisions in a meeting yourself? If any of these resonate, I encourage you to become aware of whether you are a barrier or an enabler to psychological safety in your team.

Encourage a learning mindset within your team

If the team's focus is on learning rather than judging, on encouraging rather than marginalising, then we can enhance the psychological safety of the group. A team with a culture of learning is comfortable with raising difficult issues, challenging the status quo and asking questions. They are comfortable with feedback from both inside and outside the team. So, encourage questions, see failure as an opportunity to grow, and run experiments and learn from them.

Show your vulnerability

Do you find it easy to show vulnerability in front of your team members? I have seen it done well when a senior leader I worked with spoke about the challenges they were facing, their development areas and their struggles combining a busy work load with a busy personal life. Their courage to show their real self had an enormous impact on the team. It allowed others to show vulnerability and increased the level of trust and safety in the team. Brené Brown, an expert in the power of vulnerability and trust (watch her TED Talk 'The Power of Vulnerability')[28], suggests that vulnerability is the absolute heartbeat of innovation and creativity. Without the courage to be vulnerable, it is difficult to take risks. So, start role modelling vulnerability for your team and encourage them to do the same. I discuss vulnerability more in Chapter 19.

Engage the 'no'

Oftentimes we look for consensus or to get everyone on board with an idea. When individuals or groups oppose our ideas, we seek to shut them down. Rather than dismissing or marginalising people who disagree, embrace the 'no'. Try to understand their perspective by encouraging them to advocate their views. Engage with those who disagree with you. Rather than asserting your ideas through factions within your team, work with those who disagree to better understand where they are coming from. Psychological safety doesn't mean we seek harmony. It means that we are comfortable with engaging in disagreement based on intellectual conflict rather than interpersonal conflict.

CHAPTER 14

Deep Listening

One of the things that my coaching work has taught me is the importance of deep listening. It is still a growth area for me, but it is something that I have become much better at over time. In my early days of coaching I would be thinking about what my next question would be or I'd get side tracked with a comment the coachee had made and then found I was missing what the individual was saying to me. I remember bringing it up with my own coach at the time and he gave me some very good advice which has stuck with me for nearly 15 years. He said that 'good coaching is creating a holding space for the other person to do the work'.

One of the ways we create that holding space is through deep and attentive listening. When you are not listening deeply, you are making it about your needs and not the needs of the other person. This has stood me in good stead in the coaching work that I do.

The importance of good listening was further highlighted to me when I started improvisation comedy classes. One of the most important principles of improv is listening to your partner. It sounds simple, but remember you don't have a script with improv, so as a newbie I would try to think of what I was going to say next rather than listen and respond to what my partner said. My teacher has been very good at picking up where I might talk over the top of someone or fail to respond to what my partner is saying. I feel my work with improv will help me be an even better listener. Even as I have progressed from Level 1 to Level 2, I have noticed the improvement. I talk over the top of others less and I am focusing deeply on what my partner is saying.

Many of us listen with a busy mindset. The symptoms of this involve listening for your turn to speak, finishing other people's sentences, interrupting people, fixing a problem, trying to assert your own view, jumping ahead, paying selective attention, multitasking or even zoning out. Listening with a busy mindset is an agility killer. It stops us from understanding others' perspectives, holds us to our own views, and dilutes our capacity to connect.

Let me give you an example of the impact poor listening can have.

Liz, a senior marketing executive, was super smart and understood concepts and ideas quickly. She also had a bias for action. Liz would get frustrated with her team for not keeping up with her. In meetings, she was quick to dismiss others' views as she didn't have time to bring them up to speed. When she was one-on-one she would get impatient with team members who wanted to discuss issues, but at the same time she wanted to resolve them and move forward. In collecting stakeholder feedback as part of our coaching process, I spoke to a number of her team members. Some of their comments included 'I don't feel listened to', 'I don't feel valued', 'I understand she is smart and picks things up quickly, but I feel her impatience and frustration, and so I don't bother exploring issues with her', 'I just try and get through the one-on-one as quickly as possible', and 'I can see her eyes glaze over, I can tell she is thinking of something else'.

When Liz and I first discussed her feedback, she was defensive and made it about her team not keeping up rather than her poor listening skills. We discussed the impact her poor listening was having on team engagement, capability building and diversity of thinking. We spent some time in sense making (Chapter 2) and Liz recognised that to respond to her changing environment she needed her team engaged and motivated. She also needed to tap into their thinking rather than just relying on her own way of looking at things. Liz also realised that she did this with other stakeholders, and that this weakened her ability to collaborate and make progress on key issues.

Most people think they are better listeners than they actually are. We are often not the best judge of our own listening skills.

Deep listening means being present for the other person, without judgement. Think of the best conversation you have had. What made it a great conversation? The likelihood is that you felt listened to and that someone was really present for you without judgement. Deep listening also opens you up to greater learning. You may have learnt a lot about the other person, as well as about yourself.

So, ask yourself, how effective am I at deep listening? Even better, ask others about how they experience your listening. Don't forget that it's about impact and not intention!

Ideas for developing deeper listening

Be fully present

It is nigh on impossible to deeply listen without being fully present. Being fully present means focusing our attention on the person we are listening to. It involves being fully engaged with the other person, suspending judgement and letting go of any distracting thoughts. When you notice you're not being present, bring yourself back to focusing on what the other person is saying. You can use mindfulness to help you do this. I try to focus on each word that is being said by the other person to bring me back into the here and now. When you are fully present, the other person will feel highly valued.

Focus on what the other person needs and how they are feeling

Marshall Rosenberg, the pioneer of Nonviolent Communication, discusses two components of deep listening[29]: listening to how people are feeling, and listening to what people need. What I like about this is that the focus immediately goes to the other person and requires that we communicate on more than just a surface level. It requires us to deeply tune in to what the other person is saying, how they are feeling and what's alive in them. In the upcoming chapter on developing empathy (Chapter 16), I will further talk about the importance of being an A-grade listener.

Make time for listening

Everyone is busy, and if we stopped and listened to everyone that wanted our time, we may not get any work done at all. One person I worked for in the past was very good at making time to listen. He was an incredibly busy CIO who had this way of working whereby people couldn't just pop into his office for a chat or grab him as he was on the way to a meeting. What he did well though was that when people had time in his diary, he was incredibly attentive and present to everyone in their meeting. He made me realise that you can be an effective listener if you create time and space for it.

Watch your body language

Deep listening requires body language that aligns with intent. Simple things like eye contact and nodding show alignment to intent. Using your face to align with what the person is saying is important. It may be smiling, it may be showing surprise or even compassion as they share their words with you. Watch out for deep listening killers such as eyes glazing over, looking at your watch, looking away in general and having a blank look on your face. The other one to watch out for is the dreaded smart phone. How annoying is it when you are engaging with someone who constantly looks at their phone or is distracted by the sound of a message or email coming through? Turn your phone to silent and turn it over so you are not distracted.

Chapter 15

Be Trustworthy

I recently had the pleasure of attending a seminar by Rachel Botsman, a world-renowned expert in the concept of trust, particularly as it relates to the growth of technology and digital platforms. Her book *Who Can You Trust?*[30] is a masterclass on the trust enigma, where at one level we are losing trust in institutions such as media, organisations and government, and at another level we jump into cars with strangers (Uber) or rent out our homes to people we don't know (Airbnb) and think nothing of it. It really got me thinking about the importance of trust in contemporary society.

Organisations are becoming more and more socially complex as hierarchies flatten, dual reporting relationships become the norm, working and collaborating across boundaries becomes critical, and leadership and innovation is expected at all levels and not just from the person who has the highest title.

In this complex and fast-changing world, we need to be able to trust others quickly but also be trustworthy ourselves. I am unlikely to be influenced by someone if I don't have trust in them. Without trust we are unable to show vulnerability, to have difficult conversations or to challenge an idea in a team meeting. Without trust we hold back. Without trust we show less curiosity towards others. Without trust we don't have psychological safety. Trust is the cornerstone of being human and engaging with others. We simply fail to work well with others if we don't have trust in our relationships with them.

In my work with my clients I use the following three factors to help them understand trust. Trust or trustworthiness is a combination of:

▶ Competence
▶ Consistency
▶ Concern for others

Let me describe each of these.

1. **Competence** is about the job or the task. Do you have the skills, experience, business, and operational and technical knowledge to complete the task to my expectations? Over time you build this competence through your achievements and the decisions you make. If I am engaging a plumber to do some work for me, then I am more likely to trust him/her more if they have the appropriate qualifications and have a track record of doing good work (often backed up by a referral). Competence is the easiest of the three to deliver on. It is the price of admission towards trust in the workplace.

2. **Consistency** is about the consistent positive alignment between what you say and what you do. Note that I talk about positive alignment. This is the alignment of positive behaviours and not alignment of negative behaviours. We can all behave consistently around negative behaviours. We all know someone who always turns up late to meetings or never delivers on time.

   Consistency has a strong behavioural component which is easily observed by others. It also requires the ongoing repeatability of behaviours. If I say I am going to deliver a report to my manager on Friday at 12pm and I do that, then that action sows the seeds of trust. It doesn't mean someone has full trust. It requires me to deliver on my word every time. There is a predictability to the behaviours being demonstrated. Where I see people dilute their trust in the workplace is where they over promise and under deliver. They simply make promises they can't keep.

3. **Concern for others** is demonstrating concern for the person that you are building trust with. This can cover a range of things, including maintaining confidentiality, showing a willingness to raise a difficult issue, focusing on the other person rather than yourself, being collaborative rather than competitive, showing vulnerability, acting in service of something beyond yourself, sharing credit, taking responsibility and not shifting blame. Ultimately, at the heart of trust is the concern for the other person and the value you place in the relationship. People are very quick to pick up the signals when you are focused on yourself and not on others.

If you can demonstrate each of these three trust factors, you will accelerate the trust you have with those who you want to engage with.

Ideas for becoming more trustworthy

Don't be shy in sharing your expertise, knowledge and competence

One of the easiest ways to build trust is to demonstrate to others your skills and knowledge. This can be done in many ways. You can offer to help out a colleague on a project or task (this also builds on the 'Concern for others' factor of trust), participate in discussions at meetings and workshops, offer to present wherever possible, write a post on LinkedIn, join a professional association, write a blog or get involved in communities of practice both in the organisation and externally. You might feel uncomfortable with putting yourself out there, but if your focus is authentic you will find others will build trust with you.

Seek out similarities in those who you are building trust with

One of the quickest ways to establish initial trust is to find something in common with the other person. In your initial conversations when you meet people, try and identify something you both are interested with. It might be children, art, travel, sport, or a love of food and wine. Identifying a link between you and the other person creates greater affiliation and starts the trust process. This might include sharing a little about yourself or asking questions of the other. Either way it is creating a space for both of you to find that area of common interest. In my role as a coach I have been involved in over 3,000 feedback sessions. It is a daunting process for many of the people receiving the feedback. In nearly all cases they are meeting me for the first time, and some are feeling some degree of anxiety about the feedback they are about to receive. I use the first 10–15 minutes to get to know them, and to find something similar that is going to connect us. Once I find that link between us (last year I met someone who was doing the NYC marathon at the same time as me), I use it as an opportunity to relax both of us and build some initial trust.

Show your vulnerability

This is a core of showing concern for others. Being inauthentic and lacking integrity dilutes trust. A willingness to own your mistakes, to take accountability for something that hasn't worked out, and to show your weaknesses will generate trust. Even in times of crises, always own up to your mistakes and never seek to blame others. Seek feedback and help on your ideas. This will make you more trustworthy in the eyes of others.

CHAPTER 16

Develop Empathy

When you engage with people, do you do it with an open heart and mind? Do you seek to understand where they are coming from, to understand deeply their perspective and how they see the world? Empathy is such an important part of leadership agility. It enables us to better engage others who think differently to us. It enables us to navigate through conflict. Ultimately, empathy is a fundamental part of relating and connecting to another person.

There are a number of different definitions of empathy, but, at its heart, it is about stepping into the shoes of another to accurately perceive and/or feel the experiences or emotions of another person.

I had a powerful insight around empathy recently when I was living and working in Bali. I was co-working with a bunch of entrepreneurs and creatives, and one weekend we decided to go to Nusa Lembongan to snorkel and dive. One of my commitments to myself whilst I was living there was to open myself up to experiences, whatever they might be. Now, all my life I have had a sense of caution and a sense of unwillingness to do anything risky. When we arrived, most of the group hired scooters (as you do in Bali). I was in two minds. There was fear and cautiousness, and a sense of anxiety. I hadn't hired a scooter in the two weeks I had been in Ubud, so why would I change now? The fear and anxiety were driven by a limiting belief (a belief that holds you back) that I can't do this, and I am incompetent. A feeling I try to avoid! In other words, I just wanted to play it safe. But I decided to lean into my nervousness and try the scooter. One of my fellow travellers instructed me on how it works and away I went. For the first couple of rides I was cautious and a little slow, but as I gained experience I became more confident and competent. So much so that on the second day of our trip I went out riding by myself. I am so glad that I was able to step outside my comfort zone and learn.

When I later reflected on my emotions, the level of anxiety and my limiting belief, I was deeply moved to think of my clients and the anxiety they must feel when I ask them to step outside their comfort zones. At times I have been very rational and cognitive about it, without stepping into their shoes to know how they might be feeling. I also learnt that showing support, care and encouragement (dare I say, empathy) for someone stepping outside their comfort zone is so important. My fellow travellers were brilliant with supporting me, waiting for me and encouraging me (thanks MJ and Maxime!). It was such a wonderful lesson for me around empathy. It has allowed me to create a safer and more connected space with my clients, to enable them to do deeper work. This has been a gift.

Our capacity for empathy starts at an early age, but can become diluted over time as our experiences lead us into focusing on ourselves. Self-absorption is an empathy killer.

Roman Krznaric[31], a writer in the field of empathy, distinguishes between two types of empathy:

1. **Cognitive empathy.** This involves a willingness to consciously know and understand how another person is thinking and feeling. It can also be referred to as 'perspective taking'. I can

cognitively empathise with a colleague who is frustrated with the lack of preparation a coaching client is bringing to the coaching session. I sense and understand the frustration, I know where they are coming from, but I may not feel the frustration that they feel.

2. **Emotional empathy.** Also known as 'affective empathy', Krznaric describes this as the 'sharing or mirroring another person's emotions'[32]. This sharing and mirroring of emotions enables us to feel what another person is feeling. It requires the ability to tap into the same emotion that the other is feeling. It can include both positive emotions, such as joy, and negative emotions, such as frustration. This ability to share these emotions enables us to connect with others beyond a superficial level.

In these two types of empathy, I found that the first was much easier for me. I have traditionally been a cognitive type of guy that deals well with intellectual discourse, but my affective empathy 'muscle' has been less developed. Like any muscle you can work on it and strengthen it. I know developing my empathy muscle is challenging my growth, and with my coach I have used some of the ideas on the next page to make progress. What nudged me towards this development work was the desire to connect and relate to people who were different to me. I wanted to better understand others and seek a deeper connection. This plays out in my personal life as well. The willingness to build affective empathy has helped me connect with those people who are important to me in both my professional and personal life.

So, what does showing empathy look like?

It may mean different things to people, but in my experience highly empathic people do the following:

- ▷ They are fully present when they engage with others.
- ▷ They are deep listeners.
- ▷ They show genuine curiosity and care towards others.
- ▷ They suspend any judgements and prejudices.
- ▷ They open up and reveal their own vulnerability.

Showing empathy is not easy for many people, particularly in the work environment. I encourage you to develop your empathy muscle by thinking about the qualities above. Pick one you would like to practice more and notice the impact it has on the connection you have with another person.

Ideas for developing empathy

Start by showing empathy and self-care towards yourself

One of the main reasons why people struggle to show empathy is that they struggle to show empathy towards themselves. Self-empathy involves listening to your own unmet needs and treating yourself with compassion and kindness. I coached someone recently who was struggling with empathy and also self-empathy. He had a recurring knee injury for a number of years that stopped him from running. I asked him when he last saw a health professional about it. He replied that he hadn't as he was too busy. He wasn't creating time for exercise and was carrying weight. I asked him what he could do to show more empathy and compassion to himself. Creating space for exercise and seeing a health professional are two examples of self-empathy. It is saying that I matter. If we can't show ourselves empathy, how can we expect to know how to show it to others? Empathy towards self can be done in a number of ways. It might include showing yourself kindness rather than being hard on yourself and setting yourself uncompromising standards. It may include expressing your needs, rather than suppressing your needs. In our busy lives we are often not in touch with what we actually need, nor can we express those needs. Using your journal, write down your needs, find your internal empathic voice and think about how you could practice self-care. What things could you do to meet those needs? If you struggle to show empathy and compassion towards yourself, I suggest you work with a coach or therapist to help develop strategies to do this.

Become a deep listener

A key to empathy is to listen without judgement to someone else. When you listen to someone's backstory, you can't help but have empathy for them. We are not talking about listening for your cue to talk or to fix the problem. We are talking about the deep listening where you are fully present to what the other person is saying. In Chapter 14 (Deep Listening), I refer to two key things when listening. The first is to listen to how someone feels.

What emotion are they expressing? Are they frustrated, angry, sad or delighted? Are their words congruent with their emotions? People may say that they are fine, but their emotion says something else. Deeply listen to hear their emotion. The second is to listen to what they need from you. Do they need you to solve a problem, share their frustration or simply listen to them? To be a deep listener, stay present and really tune in to what they are feeling and what they need from you. Deep listening is a great way of showing empathy towards someone else.

Be mindful of defensiveness, biases and judgements

Are you prone to judging people? One thing that stops empathy in its tracks is passing judgement or stereotyping people and situations. Once we start judging and stereotyping people, we stop showing curiosity and care towards them. Similarly, if you are busy defending your position, you are making the conversation about you rather than the other person. If you want to develop more empathy, I encourage you to identify stereotypes and judgements that stop you from walking in the shoes of others. When you are communicating with others, suspend judgements on what they are saying or feeling.

Try and walk in the shoes of another who is different to you

One of the best ways to develop empathy is to walk in

the shoes of another person who is different to you. Who is different to you, and how could you better understand their world? What is it like to be a working mother with three young kids? What is it like to be refugee? What is it like to be homeless? Developing empathy requires us to walk in the shoes of those who are different to us and to see the world from their perspective. When I was living in Bali as part of my sabbatical, one of the things I did was spend time with locals to better understand what it was like to live in Bali. I could have lived the life of an expat, but I wanted to better understand the culture and social mores of the Balinese: how they viewed gender, religion, tourists, family and work. I went to workshops and chatted one-on-one with the locals. There is much to be gained from the Balinese culture and their belief in Tri Hita Karana: a philosophy that locals follow so they can live in harmony with their community, their spirituality and their environment. So, what are some practical things you could do to walk in the shoes of others? You could try volunteering (contact organisations such as the Red Cross or www.volunteeringaustralia.org for volunteering opportunities). You could watch documentaries. You could connect with the Indigenous community. You could do board work for a not-for-profit in an area that interests you. Whatever you try, find something that connects you with difference.

CHAPTER 17

Embrace a Different Perspective

Have you ever had conflict with another person and you simply couldn't understand why he or she just could not agree with you? It seems so obvious, right? 'What is the matter with you? Can't you see that I am right?' This chapter is all about being able to embrace, or at least deeply understand, a different perspective to your own.

When we dismiss groups or see them as inferior to our own, we immediately dilute diversity. One example of this is the bad rap Millennials get from Gen X and Baby Boomers. They are described as lazy, entitled and rude. They can't commit to a job. They want to be at the top of the tree now and not do the hard yards. Sound familiar? This stereotyping and generalisation dismisses one group and suggests that our generation is right. However, when we do that, we miss the richness that millennials bring in terms of their perspectives. There are many positives, such as their adeptness with digital and social media, their emphasis on meaning and purpose, and their entrepreneurial and creative skills. They see the world differently because their problems are different to those of Baby Boomers and Gen X. We should be leveraging their difference and not dismissing it.

When we deal with different people, stakeholders or groups, we have competing truths. We often struggle to see the truth because we are wedded to our own perspective, and we see our own perspective as truth. We filter the world through our experiences, upbringing, values, assumptions, judgements and biases, to create a world view and to us it is truth.

At the same time, another person has their own world view. They too have biases, assumptions and judgements about how things are. In their mind this is their truth, just like the way we see things is our truth. Essentially, there are competing truths.

Let me provide an example. A crying child in the supermarket can elicit compassion from one onlooker, and judgement about the poor parenting from another onlooker. In the same situation, the onlooker who showed compassion may be a mother of teenagers who knows only too well what it was like years ago when she was tired from little sleep, walking around a supermarket with a child in tow who would not stop crying. She was able to step into the parent's shoes without judgement. The other onlooker, who had not had children, looked on with judgement, questioning why the father wasn't controlling the crying child. Both onlookers had the same experience, but their different perspectives influenced how each of them saw that experience.

In the workplace there are many situations where we experience events differently to one another. When we take positions that are different to others, we see our perspective as the truth, rather than simply our own perspective.

What stops us from embracing another's perspective? Pride? We may be apprehensive that seeing the other's perspective will lead to us losing the argument . . . or, worse, being placed at a disadvantage. But the true value of understanding another perspective lies within seeing more of a situation and therefore being able to make better judgements, not only for ourselves but for the other person too.

If we want to engage with others more effectively, then we need to surround ourselves with colliding perspectives from people who see the world differently to us. The more we bump into people with a different world view, the more we challenge our own thinking, and allow the possibility of seeing the world in new and exciting ways. If we can integrate different perspectives and see the grey in issues rather than just the black and white, we will be better able to cope with complexity and embody agility. During my 2019 sabbatical, I had the pleasure of attending a yoga and meditation retreat in Thailand and a co-working retreat in Bali. At both retreats I managed to meet people whose backgrounds, experiences and world views were different to mine. Some of the people I met would not normally exist in my world. The chance to spend quality time, deeply connect and engage in some challenging conversations enabled me to expand my world view and to embrace the different perspectives that were available.

Ideas for embracing different perspectives

Get curious!

When you find yourself judging or making assumptions, then get curious. Curiosity enables us to stay open. Judgement leads to closure. It is hard to understand different perspectives if we are in closure mode. If you find that you disagree automatically with someone else's perspective or position on something, then show curiosity. Start with asking more questions, or share your own biases and assumptions and get the other person to share theirs. There are many complex issues or positions we disagree with. You only have to read the newspaper to see opposing positions on immigration, refugees, climate change, abortion, the role of government in our lives, and whether we reduce deficits through increasing tax or decreasing spending. When it comes to these issues, people can hold on to their perspectives tightly. You can expand your perspective by trying to see these positions through the eyes of other people first, before judging them. This sounds easier than it is. If you can understand the actions of others, if you can feel their motives within you, then you can truly say that you see their perspective. Otherwise there remains a certain amount of ignorance, which ultimately leaves you with a singular and narrow perspective. Of course, this doesn't mean you need to agree with them, it simply means showing a willingness and a skill for understanding them.

Switch perspectives

I remember having a disagreement with a colleague many years ago about whether we should give participants their 360-feedback report (a confidential report that collects and collates the feedback from a range of people who know the participant) prior to their debrief. We were both arguing for the benefits we saw for our own position on this issue. He then suggested we both switch perspectives by arguing the benefits of the other's position. I argued for his position and he argued for mine. It gave us both a real moment of clarity by seeing the other person's view. I felt like I better understood where he was coming from, and in the end I was able to see his position was actually a better one. So, if you are in a disagreement with someone, try and switch perspectives. You might find you reach the optimal solution faster.

Peer coaching

In my workshops I get participants to engage in 'peer coaching'. This form of collaborative coaching focuses on a participant bringing a real issue they are grappling with to the group. They present their issue and then listen to the group as they process what they heard, offer their perspectives of what might be going on, and suggest potential solutions. It is an eye opener for the person presenting the issue to hear multiple perspectives on what might be happening. They initially want to defend their view, but are gently encouraged to stay open and curious to what they are hearing. You could do the same exercise with a couple of peers over a coffee. Present your issue and get them to provide their perspective of what is happening and what you could do. Make sure you give them all the facts of your situation and make sure you're not defensive. You will gain enormously from seeing someone else's perspective.

Practice both/and thinking

The American novelist F Scott Fitzgerald observed that 'the test of a first rate intelligence is the ability to hold two opposed ideas in the mind at the same time and still retain the ability to function.' This sums up the idea of 'both/and' thinking, which I referred to in Chapter 8. I want to allow some nuance when it comes to applying this thinking to embracing and understanding different perspectives. In this context, 'both/and' thinking is the ability to hold on to two competing or opposite views. It allows us to understand and agree with a perspective whilst simultaneously believing something that competes with this perspective. For example, I might be an atheist, but believe that individuals should be able to practice their faith without judgement. Another example: I might be disappointed in the policies of the government of the day but accept that the democratic processes that led to that government is something to be proud of. If we can adopt 'both/and' thinking, we can start to better appreciate perspectives that might be different to our own.

Chapter 18

Embrace Productive Conflict

Conflict is inevitable and a natural part of life. In organisations, teams and communities, we bump up against people who have a different world view and at times have competing interests to our own. If we want to make progress on important issues, it is more than likely that some individuals will experience some form of loss. A good example here in Australia is that the current Federal Opposition is proposing tax changes that would take money away from retirees and give that money back to services such as health and education. The broader community may see this as a gain, but retirees see it as a loss. When people fear losing something that is important to them, they can get passionate and protective of their ideas, their beliefs or their patch. This is where conflict occurs. When we manage conflict ineffectively it can lead to people sticking rigidly to their views, relationships breaking down, elephants staying in the room, and progress on difficult issues stalling or stopping altogether.

Conflict can, however, be highly productive – it can highlight the similarities and differences of ideas, provide an opportunity for generating better alternatives, and help increase clarity of context. Constructive conflict provides an opportunity for new ideas, for changing hearts and minds, and for strengthening relationships. It encourages mutual understanding and a willingness to collaborate in service of a collective purpose. We are more effective if we manage conflict in the positive spirit of collaboration and mutual gain.

Having said this, too much conflict can also have a negative impact on a team or organisation. It may result in too much discussion and not enough action. People may see excessive conflict as a 'sport' rather than a genuine tactic for moving forward. If there is too much heat in the system, people can disengage. The trick is to get the right amount and the right type of conflict.

When we talk about 'the right type of conflict' we are really referring to 'productive conflict', which is conflict and debate around ideas, issues, and concepts. Economist Linda Hill, from Harvard Business School, and her colleagues refer to productive conflict as 'creative abrasion'. In their words 'creative abrasion is a process in which potential solutions are created, explored, and modified through debate and discourse. It can and often does involve heartfelt disagreement or heated argument.'[33] Productive conflict is a critical component of innovation. It helps sharpen ideas.

I worked with a team that became very good at orchestrating productive conflict. If they felt they were circling an issue or avoiding the real conversation, the leader of the team would name what he was seeing. This would jolt the team into sharing what they were avoiding, and leaning into debate they needed to have. When they went into that debate, they followed three simple rules: These were:

1. Listen without judgement.
2. Treat every opinion as valid.
3. Don't be defensive.

These rules enabled them to lean into productive conflict.

If you are going to orchestrate conflict around an issue, then the issue needs to be material or a game changer. It might be about breakthrough innovation or value-adding for the customer. Productive conflict is much easier if it is based around a noble intention.

When I talk about productive conflict, I am not talking about interpersonal conflict – where conflict is much more personality-based and negative. This is also important to embrace, as interpersonal conflict opens us up to learning about ourselves, our values, beliefs and emotional triggers, as well as the values and beliefs of others we are in conflict with. When we are triggered by someone and have that 'below the neck' reaction, it can lead to tremendous learning. I do recommend the management of interpersonal conflict, but in this case we are talking about conflict around ideas and issues.

Embracing productive conflict leads to greater agility. It enables individuals, teams and organisations to tap into a diversity of perspectives and ideas, which can lead to making progress on important issues. If productive conflict is embraced in line with a shared purpose, organisations will seize more opportunities than not as they respond to a changing environment.

Ideas for embracing productive conflict

Cultivate psychological safety

In Chapter 13 I explained the importance of psychological safety. Without a sense of safety, people are unlikely to offer an alternative view or perspective for fear of repercussions. People may not surface conflictual interpretations for fear of being seen as negative. If you create an environment where people are non-defensive and feel comfortable in sharing a different perspective, then this can help to make progress on important issues the team is facing. Some of the ideas below will help create psychological safety. You could also refer back to Chapter 13.

Think about the bigger picture and shared purpose

Unproductive conflict is likely to occur when individuals are pursuing their own agenda, asserting or defending their view, or protecting their patch or ideas. Productive conflict occurs when the debate about ideas happens within the spirit of a shared purpose. This purpose might be innovating for the customer or making progress on an issue we care deeply about, such as climate change, homelessness or gender equality. If there is a willingness to put a shared purpose at the heart of your discussions, then conflict becomes more about making progress on that shared purpose rather than protecting individual views and positions. Some questions I like to ask a team who want to engage in productive conflict include:

- What is the purpose of our discussion?
- What are our shared needs?
- What is important that we make progress on?
- What are we willing to let go of to make progress on this issue?

Initiate conflict

One way to embrace productive conflict is to surface it. A peaceful and harmonious workplace can actually be a negative for an organisation. It stifles innovation and creativity. An intentional focus on initiating conflict or 'raising the heat' can encourage a team or a group of stakeholders to look at the real issues. Initiating conflict might include acknowledging an elephant in the room, asking tough questions, raising conflictual/challenging interpretations (see Chapter 6) or being provocative in a constructive way. We don't recommend initiating conflict as an opportunity for sport, but as part of a broader collective purpose that benefits everyone.

Create a holding space or container

A holding space or container refers to the boundaries around the environment in which groups can interact around a shared purpose. These boundaries might include the membership of the group, time limits, the allocation of roles and physical space. Boundaries will also include ground rules for how the group debates issues. For example, confidentiality, suspending judgement whilst listening, and not attacking or marginalising other individuals who put forward an alternate view. This holding space links back to psychological safety, discussed in Chapter 13, which encourages the team to enter into productive conflict in the knowledge that there are boundaries that make it feel safe.

Overcome your aversion to conflict and see it as natural

There is something about the word conflict that sparks anxiety and trepidation in people. Conflict is a natural part of any system where there is different world views and perspectives. So try not to be defensive. Don't see it as personal. When you are in conflict with someone, think about your learning and how you could better understand that person's perspective. One way I look at conflict is that by resolving it there is a likeliness that it will lead to a stronger and deeper relationship.

CHAPTER 19

Embrace Your Vulnerability

This is one of the hardest chapters for me to write, as one of my own development areas is being vulnerable. We all have areas for growth, and vulnerability is mine. The path to my struggle around vulnerability is a long one and probably similar to others. Like many men my age, I was brought up not to share my feelings. The school system was all about measuring academic intelligence and sporting achievement, and asking for help or being vulnerable was a sign of weakness. My work roles further emphasised the importance of performance and achievement, and it seemed there was no room for failure. I remember working in the consulting division of a Big 4 firm, where it was drummed into me that you needed to always be seen as smart and knowledgeable in front of the client. This was over 20 years ago, so things may have changed.

What struck me about this as I went through my own coaching process a few years ago was that my professional life – and to some extent my personal life – was built on appearances: being seen to be in control, intelligent, unfailing, strong, knowledgeable and competent. It was better to be smart than to show weakness. It was better to know than to not know. I was the guy with my armour on each day.

What was the result of maintaining those appearances? It impacted on my relationships both professionally and personally, as I tended to gravitate to people who were more like me and closed myself off from others, and I measured my success by what I achieved, rather than a balance between achievement, relationships and personal growth.

Over the past six or seven years, certain experiences have highlighted the importance of vulnerability both in terms of my work but also in terms of my own development. The first was viewing Brené Brown's TED Talk called 'The Power of Vulnerability'[34]. This video is one of the 10 most watched TED Talks of all time, and in it Brown discusses the importance of embracing your vulnerability, being human and authentic, and not hiding behind any appearances. To allow people to see who you are rather than who you want them to see. Brown defines vulnerability simply as 'uncertainty, risk and emotional exposure'.

I delved further into this topic and read her book *Daring Greatly*[35], which highlighted to me the importance of courage and risk in being vulnerable. This came about at the same time that I attended a group dynamics workshop as a participant, which again emphasised the impact that vulnerability has on creating meaningful connections and bringing groups closer together. Like many people, I thought that in order to be vulnerable you needed to have trust and feel safe, but my insight was that my vulnerability and the vulnerability of others *created* safety and trust.

I am still a work in progress, after years spent needing to be competent and smart. What I can now see is the importance of vulnerability in relating and connecting with people.

Let me give you an example from my work. Recently I was co-leading a twelve-month leadership program with a group of executives. In the first workshop, I noticed one of the participants, Adam, wasn't giving of himself compared to other participants in the program. When discussions got a bit deeper or the attention was on him, he would crack jokes or find a way to deflect attention.

In a coaching session a few weeks after the workshop, I observed that Adam was reluctant to share anything personal and was either unwilling or unable to articulate his development areas. It felt to me that revealing anything about himself was hard for Adam. I didn't bring it up at the time as I wanted to collect more data.

In Workshop 2, a couple of the participants called him out on telling jokes and lightening the conversation when it wasn't appropriate to do so. I could see he was shocked (although others may have seen it as indifference), and at the end of the day I took him aside to make sense of his emotions. He revealed to me that sharing weakness was frowned upon growing up. He was emotional as he shared stories from his youth and the messages he received from his father about being strong and hiding weakness. I felt for him as I could deeply empathise with his story. I asked him whether he felt safe in the group, and he said that he did. I then encouraged him to take an emotional risk in the next two days by sharing something of himself.

The next day, Adam talked about why he used humour to deflect attention from himself and the discomfort he felt in sharing his weaknesses. It was a powerful moment for him and the group, and it led to a couple of others sharing more of themselves. Adam found it difficult but could see how impactful it was for him. He continued to share more of himself at appropriate times throughout the program. It led to better conversations and to closer relationships.

Showing vulnerability may not be easy, but it can have a powerful impact on the relationships around you.

So, what are some examples of showing your vulnerability?

- Bouncing a problem off a colleague
- Saying no to a request
- Admitting that you don't know
- Sharing new ideas
- Sharing how you feel
- Challenging the status quo
- Taking responsibility for something that wasn't successful
- Opening yourself up to feedback
- Moving outside your comfort zone
- Sharing your weaknesses

Embracing vulnerability helps us to be more agile, particularly when it comes to managing risk and adapting to a changing environment. It brings people closer together, encouraging people to collaborate and work together more effectively. The environments that best foster individual vulnerability are those where there is no perceived status or hierarchy. Individuals are willing to speak out, challenge the status quo, take accountability for what's not working, admit when they don't know something and reach out to others for help.

This lovely quote from Brené Brown in her TED Talk[36] highlights the importance of vulnerability when individuals and organisations are seeking to navigate complexity: 'Vulnerability is not weakness, rather it is our most accurate measurement of courage and the birthplace of innovation, creativity, and change.'

Embracing vulnerability can also help people step outside their comfort zone. There is a sense of risk when you step into uncertainty and ambiguity. Writing this book doesn't necessarily feel vulnerable for me, but launching it and getting it out into the world does tap into my vulnerability. My human reaction is to worry: what if no one buys it? Or what if people don't like it? The coach in me knows that I need to embrace the vulnerability of putting myself out there and to see everything that emerges as a learning opportunity.

This concept of embracing vulnerability is not easy for some, but taking small emotional risks and 'putting yourself out there' will create more meaningful relationships and improve your ability to influence and engage.

Ideas for embracing your vulnerability

Identify where you feel vulnerable and how you mask it

Ask yourself the question: what makes me feel vulnerable? Is it a relationship that has fractured? Is it a difficult conversation that you are avoiding? Is it a fear of failure that is manifesting itself as perfectionistic behaviour? Is it not speaking up in meetings because you are worried people might judge you? Is it trying to be the smartest person in the room rather than simply saying 'I don't know'? Work with a coach, a therapist or a trusted friend to help you identify where you feel vulnerable and how it manifests for you.

Start with the list on page 122

Showing vulnerability involves taking small incremental steps that feel risky emotionally. If you are uncomfortable showing vulnerability, then you don't want to suddenly take a massive risk. Identify something small that is doable and that won't expose you too much. If you feel that the risk is too great, you won't do it. Pick something from the list that speaks to you. Experiment with it and reflect on how you went. How did it feel? What worked? What did you observe and what was the impact? How could you go further next time?

Eliminate the negative chatter in your mind

Have any of these negative thoughts entered your head? *I'm not going to put myself out there. I'm afraid to fail. They might judge me. What are they going to say about me? What if I'm not good enough? What are people going to think of me? What if they laugh at me behind my back?* If you buy into this negative chatter, you are unlikely to show vulnerability because your mind is telling you to protect yourself. If you want to be more vulnerable, you need to engage with a positive mindset. This might include the following thoughts: *What can I learn from this? This will bring me closer to others. This will create trust with my colleagues* etc.

CHAPTER 20

Engage with Generative Dialogue

One of my coaching clients, Tina, is an experienced executive who recently moved into a similar role in a new industry. She was recruited due to her particular set of skills, and the organisation she joined was keen to leverage those skills. When I met Tina, she described the organisation as '10 years behind my previous organisation . . . it feels like they need to be brought into the 21st century'. In our discussion and through stakeholder feedback, it became clear Tina was approaching her work in the same way she had in the past. She told me about the battles she was facing, her frustration with stakeholders that were ignoring logic and highly resistant to her ideas. Meanwhile, Tina's stakeholders described her as pushy, directive and comfortable advocating her own ideas while not really listening to others.

Have you ever been in a similar situation to Tina, where stakeholders were unable to see your point of view? We think we are being reasonable, and they are not. If you are like Tina, you might feel frustrated and blocked.

In the work I did with Tina, I was able to help her understand that holding on too tightly to her view and being directive when engaging with others is the antithesis of agility. Tina needed to find a way to engage more productively with stakeholders, so I introduced her to the idea of 'generative dialogue'. To her credit, through the coaching process, she was able to reflect on what her contribution to the situation or what her 'part of the mess' was. Tina recognised that it was she who needed to change and that the organisation was simply different to her previous organisation. Tina was able to gain real clarity on her own leadership style and her approach to influencing. It reminds me of one of my favourite quotes from Carl Jung: 'Everything that irritates us about others can lead us to an understanding of ourselves.'

William Issacs, an expert in dialogue, describes dialogue as 'a conversation with a center, not sides. It is a way of taking the energy of differences and channelling it toward something that has never been created before . . . [it's] a means of accessing the intelligence and coordinated power of groups of people.'[37] The aim of generative dialogue is to shift from advocating your position to collaborating with the purpose of creating something new. Generative dialogue looks at what can be created through authentic conversation. It requires us to be open-minded and vulnerable, to listen deeply, and to let go of ego and agendas.

Ideas Ideas to help generate dialogue

Establish a shared purpose

Generative conversations have at their essence a shared purpose. It's not about my needs versus your needs; it's about *our* needs. Both parties approach the conversation with a willingness to explore something that is in service of something bigger. It requires work upfront to develop this shared purpose.

Understand and advocate your position

This involves more than simply advocating your position. It requires a deep understanding of the assumptions and biases that form your position. As you put forward your position, including the facts and evidence, be prepared to share your reasoning and any biases and assumptions that you might be making. Test those assumptions as you speak with the other person. Make apparent your data and rationale. Show curiosity in your own view rather than holding on too tightly. Showing curiosity also means that you need to be prepared to be wrong. It can also highlight gaps in your information and your knowledge. Apply humility in how you advocate for your position.

Intentional understanding of the other

In generative conversations, there is a preparedness to deeply understand the other person. Through open-ended questions and deep listening you explore the other person's views and perspective, as well as their own assumptions and biases. Show curiosity towards their reasoning, rationale and concerns, rather than making judgements. Encourage them to make their reasoning apparent to you. Check your understanding of their position by repeating back to them what you are hearing.

CHAPTER 21

Understand Your Stakeholders' World

No one ever wakes up and says they have too much influence. Well, some politicians might feel that way! Have you wanted to be more influential with someone, but found your approach wasn't working? One of my coaching clients was experiencing challenges around influencing. One of the reasons I was brought in to work with him was that he was struggling to engage and influence key stakeholders across the business. In our early coaching sessions, we identified that he had a strong sense of right and wrong, and was black and white in his thinking. His stakeholder feedback highlighted the fact that he struggled to make progress with those whose opinions differed from his. This made him less agile, particularly when it came to dealing with people he needed to engage and influence.

So how do we engage with others who see the world differently to us? How do we become more influential with key stakeholders?

I spoke about the importance of understanding your context in Chapter 5, and similarly it is important to understand the context of the stakeholders who you want to be more influential with. In their excellent book, *Influencing Without Authority*[38], Allan R Cohen and David L Bradford see diagnosing your stakeholders' world as a key element of influencing. There are a couple of key parts to this.

The first is to see the stakeholder as an ally or a partner. Too often we see the person we are trying to influence or engage as an adversary and focus on what we can get out of the exchange. We try to assert our view rather than seek to understand another. If you see the stakeholder as an ally or partner, then this creates a mindset of collective purpose and working together.

The second part is to understand what's important to them and what shapes their world. Cohen and Bradford refer to two important dimensions to better understand a stakeholder's world. These are:

1. **Personal considerations.** These are the factors that are unique to that individual. They might include things such as how they like to receive information, or what expectations their manager or peers place on them.

2. **Organisational considerations.** These are unique to the organisation and might include the goals of the organisation, the company culture, and the stakeholder's key responsibilities within the organisation.

See the table on the following page for a list of personal and organisational considerations. Note that this list is not exhaustive. In my workshops I use a template to help participants better diagnose the world of their stakeholder. They can then use that information to engage their stakeholders more effectively to achieve mutually beneficial outcomes.

Earlier in this chapter I referred to a coaching client who struggled to influence. By using the questions on the next page they were able to better understand the key stakeholder they were trying to influence. One insight they had was that status and reputation was important to the other person even though it wasn't important to my client. This was hard to let go of. My client realised that they needed to embrace this knowledge and take a different approach rather than rely on logic and a black and white view of how things should be done. This insight helped him enormously in influencing this important stakeholder.

The more we know about someone, the more options we have to influence and engage. It enables great agility as we navigate our complex social environment every day.

Personal Considerations	Organisational Considerations
How do they like to communicate? How do they like to receive information? Are they logical/big picture/detail-oriented?	What are their interests? What outcomes are they seeking?
What beliefs and assumptions do they hold on to?	How do external factors impact on the ally?
What do they value in a relationship? What gives them trust?	What are their key responsibilities?
What is their appetite for risk?	Identify how they are measured and rewarded.
What motivates them? What is important to them?	Who are their key stakeholders?
Where are they in their career? Level of job security?	What are the goals of the organisation?
What is the level of personal power? Are they well connected? Do they have strong personal networks?	What is the culture of the organisation?
What pressures are they under – What are their worries?	What are their managers or peers expectations

Ideas for understanding your stakeholders' world

Recognise that people think differently to you and that's okay

I know this sounds simple, but the quicker we recognise and celebrate that people think differently to us, the more agile we can be. The more we project our own way of seeing the world, the less open we are to understanding those around us. The world is not black and white, and most interactions are carried out in shades of grey. Recognising this opens us up to better understanding the person we are trying to engage or influence. When you interact with people, notice how they are different to you. Don't judge, just notice.

Build relationships around people and not around a task

Relationships take time, and sometimes when we work with people who we don't naturally gel with, we put them into the 'too-hard basket'. We may avoid them or relate to them based solely on the task at hand. This feels transactional and dilutes our ability to connect with them. Relationships take time, and they require us to engage on a personal level. The table on the previous page gives you some guiding questions that can help you better understand someone. One thing you might introduce is what I call a 'relationship moment'. These are those moments where you relate to someone at a personal level. It might be at the start of your interaction/meeting/catch up with someone where you talk about their day, their weekend or something that is a common interest for you both. I often share something about travel, my running or something interesting I did on the weekend. I use these key relationship moments to better connect with the person over time. I also find that they are more likely to open up further, which leads to deepening the relationship.

Become 'people savvy'

If you want to better understand, engage and influence stakeholders, then become a people watcher. Study people around you. Notice their differences. What is it that makes them tick? How do they see the world? What are their needs, preferences, emotional triggers? How have their life experiences shaped them? In group situations, notice who holds the power in the room. How do they use that power? Who dominates conversation? Who sits back? How do people engage with others? If you notice more about those around you, it can help you navigate relationships and engage more effectively.

ACTING DIFFERENTLY

One of the key agility concepts I take my coachees and workshop participants through is the magic that happens outside their comfort zone. This is where the opportunity for learning and growth happens. In a complex and rapidly changing world, our current bandwidth won't be enough to survive and thrive. If we stay in our comfort zone, we stop learning and we struggle to act differently, making us less agile, adaptable and flexible. I see it with individuals who have a preference in the way they engage with people, how they approach problems and how they motivate their team. They don't have the tools or the bandwidth available to try different things. A hallmark of acting differently is experimentation. In this context, experimenting involves acting differently and trying new behaviours often moving outside your comfort zone with a focus on learning and growth. The more time we spend experimenting and learning outside our comfort zone the greater the ability to adapt to new ways of doing things.

In my work, I've observed that people who excel in acting differently have typically had a diversity of life experiences, both professional and personal. They have been willing to learn from these experiences, which has enabled their growth. They seek the ambiguity of being outside their comfort zone and manage their emotions accordingly. They have purpose and focus on what's important and not just what's urgent. They ensure they have the data needed to make the right decisions. They have a variety of tools in their kit bag in which to respond to situations.

In this section, I will walk you through some of the practices that will help you with acting differently. This includes increasing the diversity of your experiences, opening yourself up to feedback, developing your self-awareness and managing your emotions.

CHAPTER 22

Move Out of Your Comfort Zone and into Your Learning Zone

We know that little learning takes place when we are in our comfort zone. In our comfort zone we feel relaxed, assured, competent, in control and confident. In order to grow, we must move out of our comfort zone and into the 'learning zone'. The learning zone is a place where we feel uncomfortable, less confident, a little clunky, uncertain, somewhat incompetent, challenged and stretched. It doesn't necessarily mean we will learn, but it does create the right environmental conditions for learning to take place.

Let me use an analogy to demonstrate. Imagine going to the beautiful seaside town of Torquay in Victoria (where I live) for your summer holiday each year. You might learn a little more about Torquay each visit – like when a new café or restaurant opens up – but it is unlikely you would feel challenged or stretched by the experience. You would feel comfortable with the surrounds, you'd know when things are open and closed, you'd know the events that typically take place, where the good cafés are, the shopping hours and how you fit into the environment. Essentially, you would be in your comfort zone. However, imagine if you were to travel to somewhere different – let's say, somewhere overseas for the first time, like a beach in India such as Goa. The likelihood is that you would feel challenged and stretched by this new experience. The 'newness' of different cultural and shopping norms, a different currency, the unfamiliarity of the place, the busyness and the traffic all contribute to pushing you outside your comfort zone and into a zone where learning, growth and adaptation can take place. In this learning zone, there is the stretch or productive anxiety we feel when we are growing. Willem Dafoe, the four times Oscar nominated actor, once said, 'I think on some level you do your best things when you are a little off balance, a little scared. You've got to work from mystery, from wonder, from not knowing.' This quote sums up the learning zone.

If we move too far outside our learning zone we can end up in our panic zone where we feel so overwhelmed with stress (or distress) that very little learning takes place. A good example of being in the panic zone is where you are uncomfortable with public speaking but you have been asked to make a major presentation. The important step is a step too far and can cause the individual significant stress. Rather than experience it as a learning opportunity, all they can experience is stress and anxiety. They are more than likely to turn the opportunity down.

Tom Senninger's Learning Zone Model[39] summarises the different zones that affect learning (see opposite).

In the workplace we need 'development heat' to help us move outside our comfort zone and into our learning zone. One of the best ways to demonstrate the concept of development heat is to complete the following exercise: Thinking back on your career, pick three or four powerful or impactful developmental events and experiences you've had on the job, at any point in your career, where you learnt quickly and profoundly things that you still use or

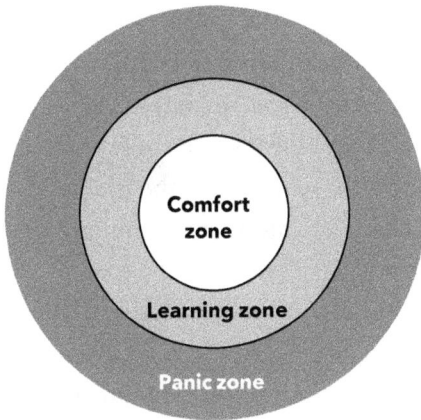

Comfort zone – where we feel relaxed, confident, certain, competent and in control. There is little opportunity to acquire new skills or behaviours in this zone.

Learning zone – where we feel uncertain, awkward, pressured, stressed, challenged and stretched. This is the zone that creates the best conditions for learning.

Panic zone – where we feel distressed and overwhelmed. This is a zone where little learning takes place

do today to do your job better. Write a summary of the experience, what you learnt, what made it powerful and what emotions you experienced at the time.

When you complete this exercise, read back over what you wrote and identify the themes, patterns and similarities of your experiences.

Did you feel stretched? Were you outside your comfort zone? Were you thrown in the deep end? Was either success or failure a possibility? Were you being watched by people whose opinions counted? Was there high stress and pressure? If you answered 'yes' to many of these questions, the likelihood is that you had some powerful experiences that involved plenty of development heat. The development heat is the stress, pressure and stretch you feel when you are learning something new.

It is the stretch or the 'heat' from these experiences that enables us to learn and, in many cases, learn quickly. I remember a time early in my career when I ran my first training workshop and did little in the way of session design, thinking that I could just wing it. I came out of the first day embarrassed that my sessions didn't hit the mark, but also aware that the participants had disengaged during the sessions. The stress of that experience resulted in me acquiring the design skills needed to perform successfully in future training workshops. It was a powerful reminder of the importance of getting the design right prior to getting in the training room. This lesson still serves me well today.

In my experience, individuals who consistently get development heat into their lives, frequently push themselves into their learning zones, and are willing to learn from those experiences are well on the way to developing leadership agility.

Ideas for getting more development heat into your life

Do something you know very little about

Development heat often occurs in first-time experiences. Those times where you don't know what you don't know, where you have to observe others to learn, where you need to throw yourself into the experience and where you might have to engage people who view the world differently to you. What's critical is that the activity is new and important to you. If you feel as though you want to give up, ask yourself what you are meant to be learning. I do this every time I am outside my comfort zone. I see it as an opportunity to learn. Some examples might be learning a language, doing improv comedy, signing up to run a half marathon, learning the guitar or attending a pottery class. One of the things I am doing as part of my sabbatical is taking singing lessons. I know this will be a stretch for me! I have no idea if I can sing, but I want to try it.

Do something that has a chance of success or failure

Deliver a presentation. Prepare a board paper. Conduct a difficult conversation you have been avoiding. Volunteer to lead a project. Choose anything that has the potential of either success or failure. There is nothing quite like the productive anxiety that comes with the potential of failure. I encourage you to focus on success, but also view any hint of potential failure as an important motivator. Make sure you have a growth mindset as you do this.

Do something that is closely watched by those whose opinions are important to you

One way of getting development heat into your role is to do something that is under the spotlight of others. Do you remember those times when you were working on something that was closely watched by key stakeholders? Let's face it, we all want to impress key people, but, at the same time, we don't want to create an unfavourable impression or be judged negatively. This generates more heat, so volunteer to work on something that stretches you and puts you in the spotlight of influential people.

CHAPTER 23

Be an Experimenter

One of the myths of development is the concept of rapid personal transformation. In my 20 years working as a coach and a leadership development practitioner, I have never seen someone truly transform in a short space of time. Developing, growing and evolving are usually the product of small, incremental changes and actions that happen over time, in line with an overall goal.

You will note that in Chapter 1 I talked about the importance of observation and sense making (creating meaning and gleaning insights from your observations). Whilst both of these stages are important, without an action or an attempt to try something different, all you are likely to be doing is building self-awareness, with no tangible growth.

One of the keys to personal development is experimentation. It is so important that you may recall it is one of my 'rules of thumb'. Experimentation is a form of experiential learning where an individual tries something different to what they normally do and then puts in place a reflective process to learn from it. This chapter focuses on experimenting and testing.

We know changing or developing a skill or behaviour is not easy. If it was easy, I would be out of a job! Change is hard. There are two key ingredients for success:

▶ You must have the *willingness* or motivation to change.

▶ You must have the *ability* to implement the change.

One of the things that makes change hard is when people make it bigger than it needs to be. This inhibits motivation and willingness. If we perceive that the change is too big, then it becomes too hard and we give up. Imagine if you weren't a runner and then you committed to doing a marathon in 16 weeks. That is a big ask, and the likelihood is that you would give up because the goal is too demanding. To use an example from the workplace: If you had a fear of public speaking and decided you wanted to improve, you wouldn't want to commit to making a big presentation to an important client the following week.

The bigger the change, the less likely you are to commit to it. This is why experimentation is brilliant. It encourages you to make small incremental changes and learn from them, all in service of achieving your goal.

What does experimentation look like? I have developed an approach that I use with groups and coaching clients. Experimenting is based on the following criteria:

1. Safe to fail
2. Incremental
3. Actionable
4. Motivated by learning

Let's unpack this.

1. **Safe to fail.** An experiment needs to have an element of risk and exposure that takes someone outside their comfort zone, but it also needs to feel safe enough that they are not putting

themselves at risk of detrimental loss. This loss might involve their reputation, credibility, an important relationship or their job. You don't want to experiment by having a difficult conversation with your manager, muck it up and be at risk of losing your job or being marginalised. Instead, you might practice a difficult conversation with a friend or a trusted peer. There may be some loss or failure, but not significant enough to cause problems. The confidence built may lead to experimenting with a more difficult conversation with your manager in due course.

2. **Incremental.** An experiment should be small and incremental. If it is seen as too big a step for someone, they are less likely to do it. One of my colleagues calls them 'mini-experiments' for this reason. It might be as simple as turning off your phone between the hours of 6pm and 8pm when you are home with the family. It may be speaking up more in a team meeting, and just observing how you feel and what the reactions are from others.

3. **Actionable.** The experiment must be actionable, in that you can do it sooner rather than later. From commitment to completion, experiments should happen within 24 hours to seven days. They should be specific and observable. For example, say that next Monday you will raise a difficult issue with your colleague that you have been putting off. Or starting tomorrow you will meditate for 10 minutes every second day for the next two weeks.

4. **Motivated by learning.** Finally, experiments involve learning and acting differently. They don't need to be successful – in fact, many experiments aren't. They can feel awkward and fail to achieve the intended outcome. What you want to do is observe what happens for you in the experiment. The key though is to learn from it so that you can refine it and experiment again.

Experimentation is at the heart of leadership agility. The quicker we learn what works and what doesn't, the easier it is to respond effectively.

Ideas for being an experimenter

Understand what it means to experiment

Run an experiment like a scientist would: use it as an opportunity to research, test and learn. Experiments are not about getting everything right or being perfect. When I prepared for my first marathon, I ran (pardon the intended pun!) an experiment around carb loading before a long run. My approach was to test what would work for me and what wouldn't, so that when I got to the week of the race I would be better prepared. I didn't expect to get it right straight away, but took it as an opportunity to learn and refine. In the first instance, I found I overloaded, and felt heavy and lethargic in my run the next day. Through continued experimentation, I found the right amount to ingest over the three days leading up to the marathon. Experiments are about collecting data objectively with a view to improving.

Remember that experiments can be messy and clunky

If experiments are to research, collect and test data, then they can also be clunky, messy and uncomfortable. Don't worry if your attempt to experiment with a new behaviour is a little messy. You might find you fail or struggle. That's okay, it's just part of the learning process. Your aim in experimenting is to try something new and collect data on what happened and learn from it. The key is to keep persisting when you experience a setback. Too often people back away from a desired behavioural change because their experiment felt messy or didn't work in the way they intended it to. Dust yourself off and keep persisting, and, most of all, keep learning.

Bounce your experiment off someone you trust

Discussing your experiment with someone you trust helps get it out in the open, and makes it more real and harder to back away from. The person who you discuss it with can help hold you accountable for your experiment. Discussing your experiment may also help you fine-tune your implementation. Finally, when you have run your experiment, they may be in a position to provide feedback, help you make sense of your observations, and help you think about what you might do differently next time.

CHAPTER 24

Let Simple Rules Guide You

Are you overwhelmed with the amount of information you have to digest in your role? What about the demands on your time, competing for prioritisation? Do you manage a range of different stakeholders who have their own conflicting interests, needs and wants? Many of my clients are overwhelmed and working long hours to stay ahead of the game. In this environment, it is useful to have some simple rules to guide your behaviour and decision making, like the ones outlined at the start of this book. These simple rules allow you to bring simplicity to complexity.

Donald Sull and Kathleen Eisenhardt, in their book *Simple Rules: How to Thrive In a Complex World*, state that 'simple rules are short-cut strategies to save time and effort by focusing our attention and simplifying the way we process information'.[40] They go on to say that these 'rules provide a powerful weapon against the complexity that threatens to overwhelm individuals, organisations, and society as a whole'.

One of my coaching clients was trying to make the transition from being highly task-oriented to focusing on improving his professional and personal relationships. Matt was highly technical, very smart and very rational. Whilst there are some who might find being people-oriented and relational easy, this was a challenge for

Matt. At the start of the coaching process, I gave Matt his stakeholder feedback which outlined some challenging critiques of his
task-based approach. In a high pressure and fast-paced environment
(which was most of the time), Matt would revert to this task-based
style. It was his comfort zone, but it caused issues for those who
interacted with him.

To help Matt feel less overwhelmed about where to begin, we
co-created three simple rules he could apply when dealing with
people whilst he felt overwhelmed and under pressure. These
simple rules included:

- Don't multitask (e.g. be on your computer or phone) when
  talking with someone else.
- Open up each meeting with something that is not task-related
  (e.g. the weekend, sports results, a movie or exhibition you
  have seen, or an amusing anecdote about your children).
- Seek out each team member in the morning and say 'hello'.

You might think these rules are simplistic, but when you are going
against the grain and under pressure, you just want things that are
simple and practical to implement. You don't want to think too
much. Obviously, you need to approach this with some degree of
authenticity or people will see through it. This advice also formed
part of the coaching.

The purpose of these rules was to make it easy for Matt to be
more relational and less task-focused, without either thinking too
much about it or adding demands on his time. In our coaching
sessions, we talked about the application of these rules and we were
able to refine them and add to them.

Context is important, and what works for another person may

not work for you. What I find is that simple rules work for a reason. They are based on collecting data from experiences and experiments to see what worked and what didn't. Over time these simple rules are developed from repeatable experiences and can be applied to our current experience.

I am reminded of the importance of simple rules with improv comedy. As you can imagine, there are no scripts in improv. There is a sense of ambiguity and uncertainty, and you are encouraged not to plan at any time what you are going to do. What helps performers to manage this uncertainty following some basic rules or principles. One rule is 'Yes, and . . .' This rule is about responding positively to what the other performer is providing you with, *and* adding a statement that helps the scene progress. If I don't react positively then the scene can't go anywhere. For example, if one performer says, 'It's hot in here,' and you respond, 'It's not too bad,' then the scene dies. However, if you respond positively by saying, 'Yes, it is, but what did you expect when we're in hell?' then the scene has somewhere to go. 'Yes, and . . .' is a simple rule that helps performers navigate the uncertainty of performing without a script.

Ideas for letting simple rules guide you

Consistently collect data on previous experiences

I've talked about the importance of learning throughout this book. One of the elements of learning from experience is to develop simple rules that can be used when the same or a similar experience comes up in the future. For example, every time I experience anxiety about stepping outside my comfort zone, I meditate on it. I learnt this simple rule through my own coaching and it allows me to ground myself and see things from a growth mindset. It is much more effective if your rules are not based on opinions or hunches but, on learning what works and what doesn't from your own experiences. I found over and over again that meditation works for me when I am stepping into a zone of discomfort. When you do review your experiences, think about the patterns of behaviour that are emerging and a simple rule that you could apply to overcome those patterns.

Your rules need to be practical and doable

There is no point having rules that you have to think about, are too theoretical, or impossible to apply. In the situation with Matt, one of the early rules we both came up with was: Don't be the smartest guy in the room. The problem was that it was too theoretical. Matt had trouble applying a practical idea around this. It was a good lesson for me about how simple rules need to be practical and doable. If you need to think about it what it means, then it is too hard to be instinctive and natural. When we looked at converting 'Don't be the smartest guy in the room' into a practical simple rule, I suggested to Matt that every time someone came up with an idea that he didn't agree with, he was to ask more questions and get the individual to say more about their idea, rather than asserting his view that it wouldn't work. This also created space for others to advocate for their ideas rather than suppress them, and resulted in improved relationships with his stakeholders.

Bounce your simple rules off others

Similar to idea 3 in the previous chapter, it is important to get a different perspective on your simple rules or principles. When we identify our simple rules, we can be influenced by our own biases as to what works and what doesn't. I encourage people to discuss their personal principles or guidelines with those who they trust. It might be a trusted colleague or a coach. Context is important and a trusted person can help identify whether the rules of thumb will apply in one context or across many contexts.

CHAPTER 25

Know Your Purpose

Have you ever met someone who is inspired by their work, driven by their values and genuinely enthusiastic about what they do? They care about their work and the people they work with, and they demonstrate authenticity and realness in who they are. One of the biggest discoveries I have had in the past two years was understanding my purpose and aligning that purpose with action. In the coaching work I do with leaders, I observe the challenges they face on a daily basis. There are times when they have to choose between competing values, face leadership dilemmas and drive change across the organisation in the face of resistance. The importance of holding onto one's purpose during these times is an important element of leadership agility.

Purpose can apply to many parts of our lives, both personal and professional. In this context we are referring to our professional purpose. Why do we do what we do when it comes to our work? What gives us energy? Why do I get out of bed every day? What gives me strength when I am facing adversity and difficult decisions?

In Simon Sinek's TED Talk[41] and his book *Find Your Why*[42], he discusses his 'Start with Why' concept, which offers an interesting insight into how some leaders and organisations have achieved such an exceptional degree of influence. He uses Apple as an example of an organisation that's been able to innovate successfully across a range of product areas. Sinek shows how organisations and leaders are able to inspire action through aligning their actions with their purpose, or their 'why'.

He distinguishes between 'why we do', which is about purpose and motivation; 'how we do', which is about the actions taken to achieve our purpose; and 'what we do', which is the end results of our actions. He asserts that exceptional people and organisations focus on why they do what they do. I highly recommend you read his excellent book, *Find Your Why*.

This 'why we do what we do' or purpose is what drives good leadership. Action without purpose can lead to inefficiency and wastage of resources, whether they be your own or that of others. Purpose is what keeps us centred when we face dilemmas, and gives us courage when we are faced with difficult situations. Purpose comes from the heart, it gives us energy and connectedness with what we are doing.

In writing this book and working through my own personal development, I realised that I needed to do more work on my core purpose. I was able to do this through some coaching work and deep reflection. The purpose or 'why' for me is to learn and grow every day, and to help individuals and teams do the same. I truly believe that I can help my clients to learn and grow and make progress on change that matters to them. I also believe that if individuals continue to grow, then that will lead to a kinder world.

My purpose guides me on a daily basis in the work that I do. It motivates my actions, it allows me to manage boundaries, and it encourages me to be authentic and true to myself. My purpose will be different from yours. We each need to find our own work purpose.

One thing to be careful of is holding too tightly to your purpose. There is a fine line between staying true to your purpose and being an immoveable zealot. If your purpose stops you from engaging with others, then you might be holding on too tightly. Helping others see your purpose and your good intentions will help you engage with them more effectively – just don't be militant about it.

To help clarify whether you have a purpose or not, think about whether the following statements apply to you:

- ► I am always busy and never feel I achieve anything.
- ► I am easily distracted by things around me.
- ► I feel as though there is something missing in my work (and life).
- ► I wish I could make more of a difference in the work that I am doing.
- ► I don't enjoy my work, but I am not sure what else I can do.
- ► I am often pulled in different directions and feel as though I have little control.

If some of these statements resonate for you, then you may not have established a deep purpose. To help my clients get focused around purpose I ask them to think about a set of questions. These include, but are not limited to:

- ► What energises me from a work and career perspective?
- ► What gets me excited about going to work?
- ► What do I truly value when it comes to my work and my career?
- ► What impact do I want to have in my career and work?
- ► What's the core question I want to answer when it comes to my work?
- ► If I was practicing self-acceptance, what would that look like from a work and career context?

Through deep reflection on these types of questions, you can start to work through your purpose. In your journal, write down the words and phrases that come up for you in response to the questions above. Play around with the words and chat to people who know you to see if they align with what they see in you. Then reflect some more and, using the words and phrases, craft out your purpose. Save it in your journal. See page 155 for more on this.

Ideas for knowing your purpose

Learn from people you know who have purpose in their life

Think of the people in your life who love the work they do. Think about what it is about them that makes you sure they know and live their purpose. What do you observe in them? What do others say about them? What impact do they have on those around them? Chat to them about why they love their work or career. What words or phrases do they use? You don't have to adopt their purpose, but it may inspire you to think about your own.

Hold to purpose (but not too tightly)

I have been fortunate to spend time at the Kansas Leadership Center. One of their key rules of thumb for building the leadership capacity of Kansans is holding to purpose. Essentially this means that, even when challenged or distracted or knocked off course, which can happen constantly, the important thing is to go back to your purpose. This enables you to focus when challenged. This reminds me of one of my favourite scenes in *Braveheart*, when William Wallace and his fighters faced charging horses with men carrying weapons. Wallace shouts out, 'Steady . . . hold . . . hold . . . hold,' as the faces of his men show their fear. The 'purpose' in this battle was their surprise use of long, sharply pointed poles that they planned to lift just as their opponents were upon them (apologies for the spoiler!). Wallace's use of the word 'hold' communicated the importance of holding to their purpose and strategy, even in the face of adversity. We can see parallels in the workplace. When facing a dilemma, or a choice between competing values, always hold to your purpose to guide your actions and your decisions. This will stand you in good stead.

Write your purpose down

This is a simple idea. One of the ways to keep purpose front of mind is to write your purpose down and carry it with you. I keep a journal and at the start of the journal is my purpose. I refer to it every day, and it is at the front of mind when I face difficult choices, or feel emotionally triggered or challenged in my work. I will often ask myself if what I am about to do is in line with my purpose. Write it in your journal or on an index card, put it in your phone, or have it on a pin board in your workplace.

CHAPTER 26

Don't Overuse Your Strengths

There are times when I love focusing on my strengths. It makes me feel confident and competent. Strengths are great! Who wouldn't want to have strong technical skills or interpersonal skills, or strong emotional intelligence competencies such as self-awareness, composure and empathy? There is a whole movement (called 'strengths-based development') that encourages people to focus on leveraging their strengths rather than focusing on their weaknesses. We don't want to get into an argument about this approach, other than to say that focusing solely on strengths in any development process is fraught with danger. Leadership is not a menu where we can pick and choose what we want to focus on. Focusing on just our strengths is a sure-fire way to leadership derailment. Indeed, one of the key reasons why individuals derail professionally is overusing their strengths to their detriment.

I had a recent coaching engagement working with an executive who was newly appointed to a General Manager role. He had a track record of delivering results (it was a clear strength), but wasn't strong at the relational or people side of leadership. He initially struggled to connect with his team and his internal stakeholders, and his style was seen as uncompromising, direct and rational. This is where I came in! His view was that if he focused on results hard enough, then that should be enough to compensate for his poor relational style. I had to help him see that, whilst this approach may work for him in the short term, in the longer term he needed others to help deliver results. Over-relying on good results and neglecting relational skills was going to lead to problems down the track. That is one of the downfalls of overusing our strengths – it can result in ignoring other skills that are important for success in the job.

There has been a great body of research positing that over-using your strength can be a liability. Kate Ludeman and Eddie Erlandson highlight in their book, *Alpha Male Syndrome*[43], that the stronger the strengths or positive qualities we have, the more likely they are to erupt as negatives.

Let's take another example. Composure is highly valued in leaders. When applied well the leader can look calm, measured, considered and cool under pressure. There is a level of maturity that goes with being composed and showing little frustration. However, if someone overuses their composure, they may come across as aloof, reserved, detached, uncaring or unable to show emotion in appropriate situations. If you want the 'light on the hill' motivating speech, then best not to use someone who overuses their composure.

One of the reasons we overuse our strengths is that we feel in control and in our comfort zone. If you are a specialist, using your technical strengths gives you a sense of competence and confidence in what you do. What we see with many individuals is that, when they are under pressure or in unfamiliar territory, they seek to reduce their anxiety by going back into their comfort zone. They seek certainty, and one way to gain certainty is to revert back to their strengths. We often see this with mid-level leaders who are strong operationally and then get promoted to a senior leadership role and struggle with the political and strategic demands of their new responsibilities. They deep dive back into the operational running of the business to the detriment of their other duties. In my work with executives, those who make progress are those who let go of what made them successful and embrace what *will* make them successful.

Those who continue to overuse their strengths struggle to develop leadership agility. They rely on staying in their comfort zones and doing things that are familiar. Those who have developed leadership agility have the versatility and flexibility to utilise different skills depending on their situation. They are comfortable with letting go of being the expert, and learning and embracing new skills that are critical to future success. They let go of the need to rely on a few strengths and see the benefit in having a range of tools in their kit bag. This enables them to think, engage and act differently depending on the context.

Ideas for not overusing your strengths

Identify the strengths you overuse

This is the first step in ensuring your strengths don't become a liability. You could engage an accredited coach like myself to use a 360 tool like the Korn Ferry Leadership Architect® which, in addition to measuring effectiveness against a set of competencies, also measures overuse. If you're unable to engage an accredited coach, then the following exercise might help.

Strength	Weakness
Step 1 List all your strengths here. Don't be shy!	**Step 2** List all your weaknesses here and again don't be shy!
Step 3 See if there is a connection between those strengths you have and how they manifest as weaknesses.	

Are your strengths at the opposite end of the continuum of your weaknesses? This would suggest you might overuse them.

Common ones we see are:

Strength	Weakness
Interpersonal savvy and good with people	Can struggle to have difficult conversations and hold people to account
Innovative	Poor planner and administrator
Direct, uncompromising and overly honest	Interpersonal insensitivity
Intelligent	Arrogant
High work standards, perfectionistic	Micromanaging and poor staff engagement
Results Focused	May struggle interpersonally and engaging with stakeholders

Reduce the impact of your overused strength

One way to stop overusing your strengths is to reduce the impact or what I call 'noise' around the strengths that you are prone to overusing. I am not suggesting that you stop focusing on your strengths, but reducing the noise or the impact of overusing them is critical. Each strategy will depend on which strength you overuse. One approach is to find one small action that will help you improve a weakness that is associated with your overused strength. For example, if you overuse intelligence and your weakness is arrogance, then start listening more. If you have high work standards and can be prone to perfectionism, then co-create a delegation plan with your team.

Manage dualities

We discussed dualities in Chapter 8. In essence, managing a duality is about embracing the contradictory or competing elements that play out in our leadership roles. Much of leadership is not about 'either/or' but about 'both/and' situations. We focus strategically so we can prepare for tomorrow, and likewise we have to be operationally focused to deliver for today. We have to deliver results, and we have to engage and develop our people. Leadership agility is the ability to embrace these dualities and to be comfortable with the yin and yang of leadership work.

CHAPTER 27

Give Up (Some) Control

I had a young male engineer named Abdul on a middle manager workshop some years ago. He had been promoted to the role of Project Manager six months prior and was managing for the first time a team of five people. As part of the program, Abdul undertook a 360-feedback process, getting feedback from his manager, his peers and his direct reports. The feedback was not good, particularly from his direct reports. He was seen as highly controlling, a poor delegator, and not available for his team, who were overall pretty disengaged. The next day he confided in me that he had taken the feedback report home to his wife and asked her whether she had noticed anything different since he was appointed to the Project Manager role. Her response was that he was more anxious, less available, and consumed with work. Abdul was devastated with the feedback from both his team and his wife. We chatted about his need for control and how this was manifesting for him. Having become aware of it, I organised some coaching for him. The coaching process was successful in helping him understand how his need for control played out. We were also able to identify the drivers of his need to control (a fear of failure and wanting to impress) and strategies to help him let go of it. This freed him up to focus on building stakeholder relationships across the business, rather than trying to do everything for his team.

Before going any further, I should say that control can actually be a positive thing. Managerial tasks, such as setting objectives and standards, budgeting, business planning, managing performance and holding others to account are important elements of any leader's role. Without this constructive control, it would be unlikely for an organisation to be efficient in their operations.

But when an organisation is facing rapid change and complexity, it's impossible to stay in control. One of the defining qualities of complex systems is that they are fundamentally unpredictable and uncontrollable. It is not possible to control everything. We need to stay open, run experiments, be vulnerable and be comfortable not having all the answers – and this is the antithesis of staying in control.

When we talk about giving up control, we are talking about the type of control that is usually driven by an irrational belief. That belief suggests that, in order to feel okay, you need to be in control. It is one of the killers of leadership agility. I see many executives in my work who have the strong belief that they need to control their environment. This control, often an illusion, has many guises. Some of these are overt – such as micromanaging, overly directing situations, getting bogged down in the detail, not delegating or empowering team members, and displaying perfectionism. Other guises that are less obvious include playing the expert or the specialist, being defensive to feedback, needing to be right (or seen to be right), overusing strengths (more on that in Chapter 26), staying in their comfort zone, and skilfully avoiding challenging tasks.

One of the main reasons why people like being in control is because of the anxiety and emotional discomfort they experience when they are not. This is often due to a faulty belief system predicated on a fear of failure, not feeling good enough, or a worry that everything will fall apart. I hear comments such as, 'I need to control the outcome,' or 'I need to be across the detail,' or 'No one can do this as well as me'. The anxiety around these faulty beliefs is palpable and drives individuals to do everything they can to control their environment.

Being in control is hard work! It is often a constant battle of managing or avoiding anxiety and working long hours. It also has a negative impact on those around you, as you seek to control a situation or others to get the result *you* want. Have you ever worked for someone who was highly controlling? Not much fun, was it? No one likes to work for someone who is controlling. It can be very demotivating.

In my experience, leaders who are able to let go of control are more adaptable and agile. They are open to others' advice, see multiple perspectives more easily, they can empower, trust and rely on others which can result in better decisions, they seek out feedback, and they embrace uncertainty. These leaders recognise that the more senior you become in an organisation, the harder it is to control your environment. There are too many factors at play for someone to be across all of them. Still, some people try, to their detriment. It's best to get used to things not happening the way you wanted!

Ideas for giving up control

Embrace the emotional discomfort

Understand that emotional discomfort is a natural part of letting go of control. Rather than resisting discomfort and seeking ways to get 'back in control', stay with the discomfort, knowing that you are learning to tolerate the uncertainty (this is where mindfulness would help – see Chapter 10). Ask yourself, what am I meant to be learning here? This feeds into the growth/learning mindset discussed in Chapter 4.

Identify how control manifests for you

Once we start having awareness of our need for control, we can start making changes. With any behavioural change, the first key step is becoming aware of the need to make the change. In the case of letting go of control, it is important to identify how control manifests for you. Whether it be micromanaging, getting weighed down by the detail or overusing your strengths, we encourage you to become aware of how your need for control plays out. Once you know how control manifests for you, you can choose to use it or relinquish it.

Challenge your beliefs around control

One of the coaching tips I give my clients is, once you have identified those situations where you believe you need to be in control, ask the question: Is this the right thing to do, or is this just my need for control? For example, if you are prone to micromanaging your team and you are reluctant to delegate a particularly important task, ask yourself that question. In some cases it may not be right to delegate, but what you need to do is work out whether you really need to retain control or whether you are defaulting to this decision to satisfy a need.

CHAPTER 28

Diversify Your Experiences

The Center for Creative Leadership[44] conducted research over a number of decades with the purpose of understanding what differentiated successful leaders from those who had derailed. Derailed leaders were those identified by the research team as having high potential but who failed once promoted to the next level. There were many similar characteristics shared between the two groups, such as high intelligence, a focus on achievement, and no glaring personal flaws. What the researchers did find different repeatedly across their research was the importance of learning from diverse experiences.

What helped leaders to grow, change, adapt and show agility was a willingness to learn from a diverse set of experiences. By contrast, if we keep having similar experiences, then we potentially learn more about that type of experience over and over again, making it much harder to adapt to new experiences.

Let's illustrate with the example of Beata, a senior technology manager I coached a couple of years ago. Beata was the go-to person for fix-it or turnaround situations. If a division was struggling, Beata would be parachuted in to turn the division around, and she would always do a good job. She was able to quickly assess changes needed across the division and was excellent at getting the leadership team on board. She was also good at getting large divisions to focus on their core competence to deliver outcomes for the client.

How did Beata get so good at this? Well, years of doing the same thing over and over. In her early career, Beata was great at working with dysfunctional teams and turning them around. She was then assigned more projects and programs that were struggling and managed to get them back on track. Beata had a track record for fixing things that were broken and 'nursing them back to health'. She had some excellent skills that helped in these turnaround situations, but she ultimately became a 'one-trick pony'. Her words, not mine.

Her lack of diversity in her experiences impacted on her ability to develop the requisite skills to be the most senior technology leader in the organisation. Beata had strong operational skills, but wasn't strong strategically. Beata wasn't as adept in innovation, and with rapid changes in technology these skills and experiences were going to be critical. The end result was that Beata, as good as she was, was passed over for promotion.

The catch-22 was that Beata loved turning areas around and the organisation was happy for her to do it because she was good at it. Ultimately, though, this caused her to plateau. In our coaching process we worked on identifying an appropriate role that would challenge her and give her some of the skills and knowledge that needed building. Beata convinced her manager that this role was important for her career. Beata has now been in that role for two years, learning and growing and doing really good work. She is giving herself the best opportunity to take on more senior roles.

Narrowness in experiences makes you less agile and adaptable. Diversity of experiences gives you the opportunity, though not necessarily the guarantee, to learn something new. It allows you further opportunity to think and act differently.

It is generally recognised that there are four type of experiences[45] which you can learn from. These include:

- Jobs and assignments
- People-based experiences
- Training and courses
- Hardships

Below I discuss each of these in more detail.

Firstly, there are **jobs and assignments**. Many of the specific skills we need in our roles, such as prioritising, strategising and people management, are learnt on the job. These kinds of experiences can include projects, a large increase in the scale of your role, or a move into doing something that's different to what you are used to. It might be moving from an operational role to a head office role.

Secondly, there are **people-based** experiences. These might include encounters with good and bad bosses, a community of practice, peers, a coach or a mentor.

Thirdly, there are **courses and training** experiences, which might include in-house programs, massive open online courses (MOOCS), reading and social media. I find reading some of the articles that colleagues release on LinkedIn a useful part of my development.

The final experience, **hardships**, is one that we would prefer not to have, but they can be very influential in our development. Hardships can include getting fired from a role, a difficult manager or peers, or a reputational issue within the organisation or your industry. The importance with hardships is that we adopt a learning mindset, which helps overcome the disappointment and challenges presented.

Each of these types of experiences contribute to our development. The key is cultivating a career that has a diversity of experiences (although you might not want to be too intentional with hardships!). Many successful careers that I have had the pleasure of observing are ones where the individual has pursued diverse experiences that have really challenged them. Their careers have a zigzag shape rather than one that goes straight up. They think about the types of skills they need moving forward and seek out the experiences that will give them the best opportunity to acquire them.

Ideas for increasing the diversity of your experiences

Manage your career (Part 1)

Manage your career in a way that gives you more options than just being a specialist. This may sound obvious, but organisations are very good at driving efficiency, and one way of doing this is by creating specialists. If you are good at something, the organisation may keep giving you more of the same types of experiences. You start deepening your expertise rather than gaining breadth of experience. Speak with your manager about challenging assignments that take you outside your comfort zone. Discuss your career with them, focusing on how you can broaden your experiences through different assignments and projects.

Manage your career (Part 2)

Identify the competencies that are critical for future roles and that you have under developed. If you are seeking to move into a role that is more complex and ambiguous than your current one, then you need to consider what competencies and experiences you need to prepare for that role. When I am doing career coaching, I assess the person's background and align that with where they want to be in the medium to long term. If there is a lack of diversity, I work with them to identify the types of competencies they need, and the types of experiences that will help develop those competencies. Competencies should start to be developed as much as possible prior to seeking a more complex, powerful or ambiguous role. If you want to develop strategic thinking, then look for experiences that develop that capability. If you want to lead without relying on your technical expertise, then find a project or an opportunity that enables you to lead others where their technical expertise is far greater than yours. Think about what skills will be needed in the future, and discuss with your manager different experiences that will help develop them.

Seek out diverse experiences in your personal life

One way to increase your diversity of experience is to step outside your comfort zone in your personal life and explore new experiences. Travel someplace new, go to an ethnic festival, engage with an asylum seeker, get involved in a demonstration, attend a meditation retreat, eat a different type of cuisine, try some improvisation theatre, learn to salsa or attend an art class. It doesn't matter what you do, as long as it's different and takes you outside of your comfort zone. You will be amazed at what you will learn about yourself and others.

CHAPTER 29

Increase Your Understanding of Self . . . Through the Eyes of Others

Organisations that experience rapid change and complexity are made up of social systems. That is, all the people in the organisation bring their own complexity into the system. If we want to be successful in this broader system, then we need to better understand how others experience us. We can't afford our own individual system (described below) tripping us up as we try to navigate change.

In my work, I specialise in helping individuals build their self-awareness. My simple definition of self-awareness is 'the capacity to objectively understand your individual system and how it plays out in your external environment'.

There are two parts to this. The first is understanding what makes up our individual system. Our individual system contains a number of components, including our values, our preferences, our strengths, our overused strengths, our weaknesses, our emotional triggers, our needs and our world view (our belief systems, our assumptions and even our cognitive biases). These components are unique to us and highlight how complex we are as human beings.

Below is a diagram that sets out the various components that make up your individual system. It shows the complexity that you bring to any organisational system.

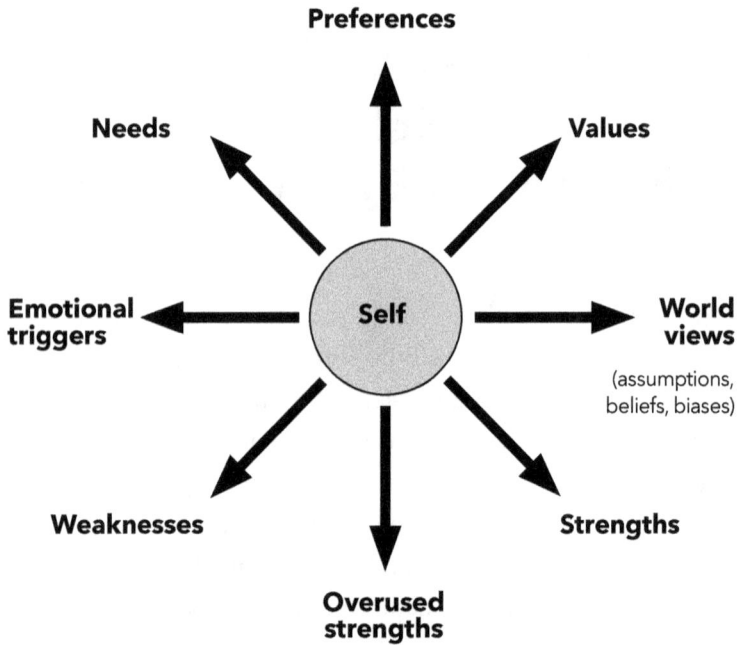

The second part of the self-awareness definition is understanding how each of these components play out for you both internally (your understanding of self) and externally (how others see and experience you).

Understanding yourself at an internal level would include your own view of those components that make up your individual system. In other words, what do *you* see in terms of your strengths, values, emotional triggers, preferences, etc.? For example, I might be aware that I have a need to be liked by others, that I value fairness, and that I am skilled in facilitating groups and understanding how people develop.

Understanding yourself at an external level involves how others experience the impact of your skills, emotional triggers, world views, values etc. This is an important distinction and highlights the importance of intention versus impact. For example, I might think I have good listening skills as I value that trait, but others may experience me as someone who interrupts in meetings or dominates a conversation with peers. In other words, my intention does not align with the impact I am having.

We increase awareness of our internal and external view through feedback and engaging in reflective practice (Chapter 1). The more we open ourselves up to feedback, the richer our self-awareness.

Let me give you an example of a coaching client I recently worked with named Ruby. When helping Ruby to understand her individual system, we identified that one of her strong needs was approval, or being liked by others. In our coaching sessions, Ruby recognised the origins of this need. She identified that her intention was to not disappoint people (something she learnt growing up), but also importantly how it manifested with her external environment. She identified her inability to say no to requests, her unwillingness to engage in productive conflict, and her tendency to procrastinate to avoid holding difficult conversations with her team. Her stakeholder feedback aligned with this, but one piece of feedback that increased her self-awareness was that her stakeholders wanted to hear from her more in meetings as they knew she had so much to offer. Due to her need for approval, Ruby recognised that she would often be quiet in meetings rather than share her opinions on things.

The work we did together was not just about helping Ruby to understand her need but also how others experienced it. Once she was able to see this, we started to work on experimenting with behaviours, such as speaking up more in meetings and stating her need to be listened to when engaging in productive conflict with her peers.

There is a flipside to this. We may have a different view of self from a negative perspective. Through our inner critic, we tell ourselves stories that create a negative view of our individual system. Our inner critic may insist that we lack competence in an area, that we are not comfortable in groups, or that we are not as smart as those around us. However, feedback from our external world can suggest otherwise. This is why understanding how people see us is an important aspect of self-awareness. It allows us to validate and benchmark our view of self. It can give us confidence to override that pesky inner critic.

Understanding ourselves and how others experience us enables us to be more agile in the moment. It allows us to deploy more effective strategies when making decisions, dealing with emotions, interacting with others and navigating our way through complex change. If you lack self-awareness, not only are you are unlikely to learn and grow, but you are more likely to have poor interpersonal relationships, be perceived negatively, and repeat patterns of behaviour that don't work for you.

Ideas for increasing your understanding of self

Understand your life story

Our experiences, regardless of what they are, whether they be good or difficult, will help shape who we are. One way to better understand yourself is to reflect back on your formative experiences and identify how each one contributed to who you are today. These experiences are likely to be from your childhood, schooling, work, sporting or artistic pursuits, travel, and any setbacks you've encountered. Grab a journal or your phone and write all the experiences down. Under each experience, discuss what happened, how you felt, what insights you have, and what kind of ongoing affect it has had on you. You could engage others to help you do this. You might like to chat to your parents, your siblings, a good friend, your partner or a coach or even a therapist. In my workshops, I do a learning lifeline exercise where participants are asked to identify key learning experiences that increased their understanding of self.

Get feedback!

In the next chapter I talk about the importance of getting feedback. Whether it be through a 360-feedback process or via a conversation with trusted colleagues, feedback can help you better understand the impact your individual system has on others. Without feedback, you may have an understanding of your inner self (how you see yourself) but not of your external self, which is how others see you. Think about what feedback you want (usually regarding an improvement you are seeking to make) and ask someone you trust to observe you and give you feedback. Try not to be too defensive when receiving the feedback. Remember that it is there to help you.

Practice reflection

One way to increase your understanding of self is to get in the habit of reflective practice as outlined in Chapter 1. You might use the following questions to guide you:

- What did I notice and observe?
- What worked?
- What didn't work?
- What could I have done differently?
- What did I learn about myself?

You can do this mentally during the day, on your drive home, or, as some of my clients do, in a journal so you can keep a track of your insights and learning.

CHAPTER 30

Open Yourself Up to Feedback

Do you find it difficult to accept feedback? In my experience, those individuals who open themselves up to feedback – both positive and constructive – have a much better chance to adapt, learn and grow than those who don't. Feedback can be very powerful. It can help us in our development journey, it can be a wakeup call or a chance to get things back on track. Whether it is formal or informal, feedback opens up the possibilities to learn more about ourselves and our impact on others.

Unfortunately, in my work I often see people closing themselves off to valuable feedback.

I have done thousands of 360-feedback sessions in the past 20 years, and I find that over 75 per cent of people show some defensiveness to feedback from others. Defensiveness is a leadership agility killer. It plays out in many different ways. See if any of the defensive scripts below sound familiar to you:

▶ They don't really know what I do.
▶ They don't understand the context of my work.
▶ I don't trust the people giving me feedback.
▶ I never received this feedback in my previous role.
▶ I have a challenging relationship with my manager/peers/ direct reports/customers/internal stakeholders.

▶ I have always been good at building effective teams, it's just this team that is dysfunctional.

▶ My job makes me act this way, I'm really not like this.

▶ This is a different culture to what I am used to.

▶ That's their perception, but it's not reality.

Many of the above can result from contextual reasons that impact behaviour, and there is no doubt that context plays an important role in how someone behaves. However, the more we focus on context, the less likely we are to focus on the nuances of the feedback and how it can help us.

Opening yourself up to feedback can be done in formal ways, such as through a 360-feedback process or a performance review, or informally by asking those around you (co-workers, family members and friends) for their thoughts. Receiving feedback can be challenging. Sometimes we don't want to hear 'negative' things said about us. It can be even harder if the feedback identifies a blind spot. A blind spot is where others see behaviours in you that you are unable to see yourself. You may not realise you exhibit certain behaviours. Without knowing this, you wouldn't be able to do anything about it. You have no doubt heard the expression 'feedback is a gift', and this is true as it gives you an opportunity to do something about it.

One exercise that I use with teams is called 'feedforward'[46], which comes from Marshall Goldsmith, a world-renowned business coach from the USA. Feedforward is like feedback, but it is focused on the future. In feedforward, each member of a team gives another member of the team two pieces of feedforward (things they could do more of moving forward). For example, one team member might say to another, 'In the future, I would like you to listen more to other voices in team meetings.' Everyone receives two pieces of feedforward from each team member, either one-on-one or in a large group (which is more confronting and only used if the teams are used to giving each other feedback). This feedforward provides a rich data set with which to work moving forward. I encourage team members to look for patterns in the feedforward. A pattern or a theme would suggest something to work on. One of the ground rules that makes this exercise so successful is that, when receiving the feedforward, the receiver is to simply and non-defensively thank the other person (remember, it's a gift!). This goes a long way to help in the development process.

As previously mentioned, opening yourself up to feedback increases your self-awareness, and this helps to avoid leadership derailment. Over the years, I've seen individuals derail in their careers due to a lack of understanding of their strengths and development areas. They either weren't given enough feedback or rejected it. This lack of self-knowledge stops them from making progress on their development and being the best they can be.

If you want to learn, grow and build your leadership agility, then you will need to open yourself up to feedback and learn how to take it on board.

Ideas for opening yourself up to feedback

Undertake a 360-feedback session

Chat to People & Culture or your line manager and organise a 360-feedback session. Pick a rigorous, evidence-based 360 tool that will give you feedback on both your strengths and opportunities for development. The tool should capture feedback from your manager, direct reports, peers and other key stakeholders. The good thing about a 360 tool is that it is usually anonymous, so people are generally more comfortable being open and honest. When you get your results, be aware of any defensiveness you might have towards the data.

Make it easy for others to give you feedback (Part 1)

If you have ever had to give someone feedback, you know how challenging it can be. It takes people outside their comfort zones. It is even harder if you are defensive towards the feedback. So make it as easy as possible for someone to give you feedback. One of the ways to do this is to thank them. Seek to understand without showing defensiveness. The easier you make it for others to give you feedback, the more likely they will be to give you feedback in the future.

Make it easy for others to give you feedback (Part 2)

Another way to make it easy for people to give you feedback is to anchor the feedback request. Don't ask someone a general question such as, 'How can I improve?', as people may not know your motivations. Try a question like, 'I would like to be more effective at building a high-performing team, what are two things I could do that would make an immediate difference?' The more you anchor your request, the easier it is for people to provide clear feedback. By doing this, you are also demonstrating self-awareness and acknowledging that you want to work on an area. This takes away any concerns they might have about upsetting or offending you.

When you get feedback, do something with it!

Let's say you agree with the feedback, but you don't do anything about it. If that's the case, then you are more likely to create a greater negative perception in the eyes of those who gave you feedback than if you had never asked them in the first place. There is a sense of perceived arrogance if one person or more gives you feedback, and you don't do anything about it. So, if you get some useful feedback, acknowledge it, process it, and do something about it.

CHAPTER 31

Make Progress on Your Own Personal Adaptive Challenge

In Chapter 5 I talked about interpreting systemic challenges as either adaptive or technical, or a combination of both. Technical challenges are those challenges that aren't necessarily easy but have a predictability about them and an identifiable cause and effect. As such, you can typically apply existing know-how and competence to resolve a technical challenge. Adaptive challenges are much more ambiguous, tend to be much harder to resolve, and often require a different mindset, a change in beliefs and a willingness to experiment in order to move forward.

The concept of technical and adaptive challenges can also apply personally. This chapter looks at how you can identify and make progress on your personal adaptive challenges, utilising the excellent body of work that Robert Kegan and Lisa Laskow Lahey have developed, particularly around the concept of 'Immunity to Change'[47]. The body of this chapter looks at how you might identify your personal adaptive challenge, and the ideas at the end discuss how you might make progress.

Have you ever tried to make change on something important to you, but it either stalled or didn't stick? I don't think I have ever met anyone who hasn't struggled to make change at some point. We see it in our new year's resolutions – whether they be about getting fitter, giving up smoking, losing weight or striking greater work–life balance. When we are struggling to make progress on a change that is important to us, we are more than likely trapped by an existing mental paradigm, or what Kegan and Lahey refer to as the 'Big Assumption'. The Big Assumption, often unknown to us, ensures we implement behaviours that work against the desired change we want to make. We commit to making the change, but we sabotage ourselves by behaving in ways that work against this change. Kegan and Lahey use the metaphor of one foot on the accelerator (the commitment to change or improvement goal) and one foot on the brake (behaviours that work against it). Essentially, we have another competing commitment that is stronger than our commitment to change.

Let me use an example to illustrate this.

I worked with Louise, who was a very competent middle manager. Louise was good at her technical work and managing her team but lacked presence and influence with senior stakeholders. Using the Immunity to Change concept in our coaching session, we identified that Louise's improvement goal was to be able to effectively influence senior stakeholders and have more presence when dealing with them. That part is the accelerator. We then identified all of the things Louise did that worked against this important improvement goal. This included, but was not limited to, keeping quiet in meetings, not taking credit for her work, not advocating for herself or her team, focusing more internally on managing her team rather than engaging externally with her stakeholders, and avoiding wherever possible presenting to the executive team.

So, Louise had the improvement commitment of being more

influential with senior stakeholders, but at the same time she was demonstrating behaviours that undermined it.

Effectively, Louise's commitment to change was being undermined by what Kegan and Lahey would call a stronger 'competing commitment'. This competing commitment is usually something we are unaware of. It is also what makes us immune to change that is important to us, hence the term.

In our conversations, we identified that Louise had committed to not putting herself in situations where she would be judged by others. So, Louise's accelerator (improvement goal) was to be more influential with senior stakeholders and her brake (competing commitment) was to not be judged by others. This made sense given that her behaviours aligned with her competing commitment. What kept this competing commitment in place was her 'Big Assumption'. Louise's Big Assumption was that if she put herself out there publicly, she might be rejected by others, and this would be devastating to her.

We all carry around these assumptions and we are often unaware of the impact they have on our behaviour. The key is to surface the assumption so you can see it and start to implement experiments to test whether the assumption is correct or not. In most cases it isn't correct, but it's so ingrained in us that we are captured by it rather than distancing ourselves from it. If you want a more detailed explanation on how to address your immunity to change, I suggest reading Kegan and Lahey's book *Immunity to Change* or attending one of my workshops where I use it to help cultivate leadership agility.

As mentioned throughout this book, leadership agility requires us to step out of our comfort zone. It requires us to extend and experiment and lean into our learning zone (Chapter 22). It requires us to be flexible with how we think, engage and act. If we are limited by our Big Assumptions, how can we improve and grow and cope with greater complexity? The more we grow, the greater the complexity we can deal with. If we are unable to make progress on change that's important to us, how can we expect those around us to do so?

Ideas for making progress on your personal adaptive challenge

Test your assumptions by collecting data

Remember, assumptions are things we accept as true without evidence. We make assumptions all the time, and the ones that hold us back most are the ones we make about ourselves. For example, Louise's assumption was that if she put herself out there she would be rejected, and this would be devastating. Louise didn't know if this was true, but believed it to be true. The important thing was for Louise to test her assumption to determine its veracity. Like a scientist, Louise needed to run mini-experiments to collect data on her assumption. One mini-experiment was to speak up more in meetings with senior stakeholders and observe what happened. Louise documented her experience and what she noticed in terms of the experience of others. This data was used to test her assumption. She continued running experiments to confirm or disprove her assumption. What Louise did really well was bring her attention to her Big Assumption. Seeing it play out enabled her to lean into more mini-experiments. I have loved hearing about her progress and her ability to get distance from her Big Assumption.

Don't look for a 'technical solution' or a quick fix

It is easy to seek a quick fix or a technical solution to a personal adaptive challenge. The reason the challenge is adaptive is because quick fixes don't work. If my improvement goal is to lose weight, then the quick fix might be to go on a diet. We know from research that diets rarely work, but we still go on them. The competing commitment might be a fear that changing lifestyle might result in less happiness. Making progress on your personal adaptive challenge requires running experiments by making changes to your lifestyle to test whether it results in more or less happiness. It is an ongoing process rather than a quick fix. Making progress takes time and can't be done through short cuts.

Recognise that anxiety is a normal part of making progress on your personal adaptive challenge

If it was easy you would likely have already done it. We know that change is difficult, particularly when we are going against the grain of hardwired beliefs. When Louise spoke up more in meetings, which had been challenging for her in the past, she felt a degree of discomfort. Likewise, you are going to feel a sense of anxiety and discomfort if you run experiments to test your assumptions. This is all part of the learning process. If you are feeling anxious, then there is learning to be gained. It's okay to feel some degree of anxiety or butterflies in your stomach, but leaning into this feeling can provide the opportunity for personal growth.

CHAPTER 32

Institute Your Own 90-Day Plan (And Weekly Plan)

In my previous corporate life, I worked with a number of line managers who would spend their days reacting, putting out fires, rarely diverting their attention from the present. They were highly action-oriented and constantly busy doing urgent tasks. Whilst there was some satisfaction experienced by getting things done, it seemed to prevent them from operating strategically or delivering on other important parts of their role, such as leading change or developing their people. They often complained that they were too busy, and claimed that 'if only they had more hours in the day' they would be able to attend to other important tasks.

When I first started my consulting career, I remember working with a client who was very good at staying 'out of the weeds' and successfully embracing all aspects of her job. I remember asking her how she was able to do it, and she talked about being disciplined about implementing a 90-day plan and a weekly plan that were linked to the key success factors of her role. These plans enabled her to focus on what was important, not just in the short term but also in the longer term. We discussed why it was a 90-day plan rather than a longer one, and her response was that any longer duration may be seen as inflexible and, with the amount of change the organisation was facing, it seemed an appropriate amount of time to recalibrate. In a fast-changing world that requires leadership agility, to not be hijacked by your environment or your current context is vitally important. To be able to stay forward-looking, even in terms of significant change, helps leaders to remain agile.

So, what do a 90-day plan and weekly plan look like?

The key to a 90-day plan is to be very clear on what the four or five key success factors are for your role. Ask yourself, what is going to be critical to success over the next 12 months? It is important that you think broadly about the role and not just about task and delivery. If you focus on task and delivery, you end up being short-term focused rather than long-term focused, and this can be an agility killer. Each role will have its own unique components, but some key success factors to think about might include people leadership, project delivery, stakeholder management, leading a change initiative, client management or peer relationships.

In my own consulting business, I have a 90-day plan where I focus on five key success factors. These include:

▶ Grow the Brand and the Business
▶ Thought Leadership (or expertise)
▶ Practice what I Preach
▶ Be a Trusted Advisor
▶ Project Delivery

By focusing on each of these categories, I ensure that I am embracing the short-term success (project delivery) and long-term success (thought leadership, and growing the brand and business). It forces me, even when I am super busy with project delivery, to focus on the long term, changing client needs and staying ahead of the game with respect to thought leadership. Writing this book is an example of thought leadership.

What's important is that you have clarity on your role's success factors. See the table on the next page for one way of doing that. When you have identified your four to five key success factors, then document three or four key achievements for each category that you would like to make over the next 90 days.

The weekly plan is simply a contracted version of your 90-day plan. In the weekly plan, I list two to three tasks in each category that align back to the key achievements in the 90-day plan. If I know I have a heavy delivery week, I still try to add one thing in each category. It is a way of keeping me honest and making progress on my overall 90-day plan. The beauty of the 90-day plan is that it allows some flexibility in the weekly plan. The key is to ensure you get something done each week across all categories. If you aren't achieving your 90-day plan, then it is likely your weekly plan is not balanced, or you're not being disciplined around what you set out to achieve.

On the next page I have developed an example of a 90-day plan. It highlights the five key success factors, and all the things I want to do over the 90 day period. This allows me to deliver on what is important to me and not just what's urgent. My weekly plan falls out of this.

Success Factors	1 July – 30 September
Grow the Brand and the Business	Speak at a client leadership conference.
	Finish a team development proposal for ABC Group Marketing.
	Prepare 'Cultivate Leadership' workshop.
	Meet with three new potential clients.
Thought Leadership	Develop six blog posts for website and LinkedIn.
	Read three books.
	Develop proposal for online coaching program.
Practice what I Preach	Attend Leadership Agility certification program.
	Attend coaching session with supervisor.
	Journal daily.
Being a Trusted Advisor	Conduct a service call with three top clients.
	Send out HBR article to top ten clients with a summary of how it impacts on their business.
	Update client management list.
Project Delivery	Deliver DEF project.
	Deliver Customer diagnostic retest for XYZ.
	Deliver Module 1 of FLP for ABC.
	Commence coaching with Bill Bloggs.
	Deliver stage 1 of 360 project for government department.

Ideas for instituting 90-day and weekly plan

Negotiate success with your manager

If you have ever read *The First 90 Days*[48] by Michael D Watkins, you'll know the importance of negotiating success with your manager. When developing a 90-day plan, I also recommend sitting down with your manager and identifying the four or five key success factors facing you over the next 12 months. You might like to think about how they align with your manager's goals and the division's goals.

Be disciplined

The key to this process is to be disciplined, and that means completing the 90-day plan every quarter (it takes me about two hours to document my key achievements for the next quarter and also review how I went over the previous quarter) and the weekly plan every week. It is easy to succumb to daily and weekly pressures and not do this, but that is the reason for doing it. By doing a weekly plan you are able to focus on what's important both in the short and longer term and not just in the here and now. I have a regular spot, depending on what I have on, every Sunday morning or evening where I set aside time to go through my weekly plan and check in with my 90-day plan. It takes me no longer than 15–20 minutes, and sets me up nicely for the week.

Reflect

An important part of the process is reflection. Prior to sitting down and preparing your next 90-day plan, make sure you review how you went against your current 90-day plan. Were you too ambitious or not aspirational enough? What stopped you achieving what you set out to achieve? How could you leverage the lessons learnt when you complete your next 90-day plan? Do the same for your weekly plan.

CHAPTER 33

Understand Your Emotional Triggers

Have you ever been caught up in a difficult conversation where you said something you wish you hadn't? Or have you procrastinated from having, or avoided altogether, a difficult discussion? Felt frustrated in a meeting when someone kept interrupting the flow?

If any of these situations sound familiar, you have experienced an 'emotional trigger' – an emotional reaction to something that has happened or potentially might happen. Understanding our triggers is an important first step in managing them, something we will investigate further in the next chapter.

One main contributor to emotional triggers is hanging on to your world view too tightly. Your world view is your socialised view of the world, shaped by your parents, your childhood, your work and your life experiences. We all have a world view or a lens through which we see the world. Our world view includes our:

▶ Beliefs (e.g. I believe that hard work should be rewarded).
▶ Assumptions (e.g. I assume that all of us are acting in service of our team priorities).
▶ Needs (e.g. I have a need to be competent at everything I do).

▶ Hungers (e.g. I have a hunger for reputation).

Often part of our world view is unknown to us, even though we carry it around with us on a daily basis. We don't consciously tell ourselves we have a hunger for reputation, but subconsciously we may hold that view.

Over the course of our lives, we bump into people who have an entirely different world view to us, which may in turn trigger an emotional response. We can also bump into people who share elements of our world view. This can also trigger an emotional response, if one feels the other is overpowering them. I worked with a team where two individuals were similar in their need for power and each triggered the other.

Our world view can be very strong and evoke a similarly strong emotional trigger when others don't see the world in the same way we do. This world view is often evoked by issues such as race, religion, gender, politics and the way we feel the world should work. It can also play out more specifically in the workplace, where our managers or fellow workmates see a professional or business situation very differently to us. For example, difficult feedback from your manager can trigger an emotional response based on the limiting belief that you are 'not good enough'. Not being part of the 'in group' at work may trigger your limiting belief that 'to be okay you need to be liked by others'. These limiting beliefs then cause a deep and personal emotional reaction that may manifest itself by you avoiding others, showing frustrations or seeking approval from others.

Understanding your emotional triggers and how they manifest is important in making progress on developing leadership agility. If we are emotionally triggered constantly by people who think differently to us, or by situations that push us outside our comfort zones, we are at risk of being hijacked by our emotions rather than responding in a way that is appropriate for the situation. Improving awareness of our specific emotional triggers means we are better positioned to manage and own them. This in turn allows us to better influence situations and people rather than react in unproductive ways.

I once worked with an executive in financial services named Geoff, who was constantly triggered in meetings by a colleague. The colleague knew how to push Geoff's buttons, which was impacting how others in the team viewed him. In essence, he was losing credibility and influence.

During our coaching, he worked out that his emotional trigger was competitiveness. He had a strong need to win, and being challenged by this particular peer evoked frustration and some-times anger. Our conversation enabled us to work out that this stemmed from a competitive dynamic established with an older brother when Geoff was growing up. He recognised that part of his world view was a 'need to win to feel good about myself.' He could see this same competitive dynamic playing out across his personal and professional life. He laughed, though he seemed disappointed, when he relayed to me that even when he played games with his kids, he still liked to win. By understanding this emotional trigger, he started to use some techniques (discussed in the next chapter on Managing Emotions) to better respond in real time. Geoff was able to better manage his emotions and increase his credibility with his peers. (As a side note, the happy ending to the above case study is that, while Geoff still likes to win when playing games with his kids, his priority now is that everyone enjoys themselves!)

Organisations are complex social environments and we are always going to bump up against people who see the world differently. In other chapters, I discuss the virtue of colliding perspectives and surrounding yourself with people who disagree with you. We will often be triggered by this, but knowing our triggers is the first step in managing them.

Ideas for understanding your emotional triggers

Keep an emotional diary

An emotional diary is a formal process of documenting your emotions and the situation that caused the trigger. It is different from the journal I have talked about, which is more free-flowing. Completing the emotional diary is more structured. If I am working with someone who wants to understand their emotional triggers, I get them to keep a diary and encourage them to complete the following table for every situation in which they experience an emotional trigger. It is important you attempt to document which part of your world view has been triggered. This helps own your emotions rather than react and blame others. We are responsible for our emotional reactions, not others.

Situation
What is the situation that caused an emotional trigger?

Emotions
What emotion did I experience? e.g. hurt, frustration, anger, guilt, sadness etc.

Strength of trigger
On a scale of 1–5, where 1 is low and 5 is high, how triggered where you?

World View
What part of your world view has been triggered?

The advantage of documenting your emotional triggers in this way is that you can start to see patterns or themes.

Look for patterns in your emotional triggers

Once you start documenting the situations that cause your emotional triggers, you may identify a pattern. Knowing what your patterns are may help you understand that your reactions are based on past experiences and don't have to define how you respond in your current situation. A woman in her early 30s I was coaching a few years ago kept an emotional diary and realised that she had a pattern of being triggered when dealing with senior men in her organisation. She felt less confident in their company, was unwilling to challenge them (even though her role allowed for that), and was deferential and compliant in her dealings with these men. Once she identified the pattern, she gained the insight that her emotional triggers stemmed from her relationship with a dominant and controlling father. A combination of counselling and coaching work led to the development of strategies to effectively manage her emotional triggers. I can proudly say that she is much more confident in dealing with senior men in her organisation and has managed to reduce the perceived power imbalance.

Seek feedback

One way to better understand your emotional triggers is to seek feedback from others who observe them. On those occasions when you appear to be emotionally triggered, ask a family member or friend to help you identify how the trigger manifests. Similarly, at work you could ask a trusted peer to provide feedback on when they feel they are witnessing an emotional trigger in you and how it presents itself. You may find you are unaware of some of your emotional triggers, so feedback from others can provide clarity.

CHAPTER 34

Manage Your Emotions

In the previous chapter we talked about the importance of understanding our emotional triggers. An understanding of emotional triggers can enable us to make a productive choice when responding to environments characterised by complexity and constant change. In this chapter, we look at how you can manage or regulate your emotions in times of constant change.

Managing your emotions is an important skill and one that requires balance. An inability to manage your emotions can result in withdrawal and isolation, unrewarding interpersonal relationships, outbursts, suppression, poor decisions and health issues.

Managing your emotions effectively can help you better respond to stressful situations. It can enable you to make better decisions, motivate your team or process the difficult feedback you just received from a customer.

You will notice I talk about effective emotional management and it is important to get the balance right. If you overuse your emotional regulation (too composed) you may appear aloof, reserved or uncaring to others. This may impede your ability to motivate your team or generate passion around your vision. Emotional management is regulating your emotions in a way that works positively for you and those around you.

One way of understanding how to better manage your emotions is to appreciate what happens in the brain – in particular, the limbic system and the prefrontal cortex. The limbic system is a set of structures in the brain that plays a key role in managing emotions. It is often referred to as the 'emotional part of the brain'. It is the place where we experience pleasure, anxiety, anger and joy. We store memories, particularly those that are emotionally significant, in the hippocampus (which is part of the limbic system). When we are triggered, the limbic system goes into overdrive. I like to use the analogy of a wild horse when describing this emotional response. It reacts quickly, is hard to catch and at times tricky to settle down.

The other key part of the brain when it comes to managing emotions is the prefrontal cortex. The prefrontal cortex is often described as the 'rational part of the brain' or 'the executive function'. It is this part of the brain where we do our planning, make decisions, undertake cognitive functions, assess consequences and moderate social behaviour. It's this part of the brain that stops you from saying something inappropriate to a colleague who has just triggered your emotions. I like to use the analogy of a jockey to best describe the prefrontal cortex. When you are emotionally triggered, you need the rational part of the brain to kick in quickly to better regulate your emotions and allow for better responses and decisions. If you are feeling stressed or overwhelmed, it is really important for your rational brain to kick in. It allows you to view a situation from a broader perspective and to see things with clarity without buying into the negative energy that stress creates.

A word of warning: You don't want the jockey (rational brain) to hold on too tightly to the wild horse (limbic system). If you are being perceived as overly rational and restrained, you might struggle to motivate or influence those around you or align people towards your vision. Emotional management is tricky and requires just the right balance to respond to the environment in a constructive manner.

When you are emotionally triggered your limbic system goes into overdrive. You can choose an impulsive reaction, which can have negative consequences, or you can regulate and manage your emotions to respond in a calm and measured manner.

This reminds me of a quote credited to Victor Frankl. Frankl was a psychiatrist and a Holocaust survivor who spent three years in concentration camps. He is credited with saying, 'Between stimulus and response there is a space. In that space is our power to choose our response. In our response lies our growth and our freedom.'

The space that Frankl refers to is where we manage our emotions in real time. We have the power to choose our response. Do we react immediately to our stimulus or do we use that space to determine a better choice? We all have the power to use the space between stimulus and response. This approach is so useful, even in the most dire of situations.

Ideas for emotional management

Practice mindfulness

I discussed mindfulness in Chapter 10. It is not my intention to do a deep dive again, as you can refer to that chapter. What I will say is that mindfulness helps manage the space that Frankl talks about. It allows you to create the space and give yourself the choice as to how you respond to situations. Whether you count to 10, engage in breathing in and out slowly, or just observe your emotions without judgement – what you are trying to do is mindfully create the space needed to respond more effectively.

Share how you feel

One of the worst things you can do when managing your emotions is to suppress them. Bottling emotions up and not sharing how you feel causes more stress, anxiety and physical health issues. Experiencing emotion, whether that be anger or frustration, is normal. Reacting to those emotions through outbursts is generally considered not okay in the workplace or, in fact, in any relationship. What I recommend to the people I coach is to share how you feel by labelling the emotion, but do so as calmly as possible. You might say something like, 'I am feeling frustrated with how this meeting is going,' or, 'I feel really disappointed in that decision.' The aim is to express how you feel in a way that is congruent with the emotion you are experiencing, without impacting negatively on the system around you.

Switch on your rational brain

Switching on your rational brain is another way to dilute the arousal of your limbic system. The quicker you get in touch with the rational part of your brain, the more choice you have in how to respond. One way you can do this is by simply identifying the emotional sensation. Another way might be to give the emotional sensation a metaphor. If you feel yourself getting angry, you might use the metaphor that the 'kettle is about to boil'. Labelling an emotion through metaphors can activate your rational brain and decrease arousal in your limbic system. In other words, describing your emotion in a word or two can reduce the power of the emotion. One technique I encourage my clients to use is to rate on a scale of 1 (low) to 5 (high) how strong their emotion is, and to rate on a scale of 1 (low) to 5 (high) how much they want to react to what has triggered them. This is what helped Geoff in the previous chapter. It helped him to create the space needed to better respond to his colleagues. Going through this process in real time allows you to tap into your rational brain and gives you greater choice in how you respond.

CHAPTER 35

Unleash Your Creativity

Do you admire others who appear much more creative than you? They might be a friend who can write music, or an artist whose paintings you enjoy, a parent who is a wiz in the kitchen, or even a colleague who always comes up with lots of good and unique ideas. I occasionally watch *MasterChef* and admire not just the ability of the contestants to cook, but their ability to be creative under pressure in order to impress the judges. I meet people in my work who would love to be more creative but don't feel they 'have it in them'. One of the reasons why people dismiss their creativity is that they think of it as something bigger than it is. They see it as some innate quality that others have and they don't have.

First, let's start with what creativity is. The simple definition that I like is that 'creativity is novelty with purpose'. In other words, there is a uniqueness or newness in an idea or concept that adds value. This definition lends itself to viewing creativity through two lenses.

Firstly, there are those who see creativity as synonymous with originality, genius and uniqueness. Those individuals, often seen as creative geniuses, are able to advance their field through breakthrough ideas or approaches. Think Virginia Woolf, Banksy, Frida Kahlo, Bob Dylan and Steve Jobs.

The other school of thought is that *anyone* can be creative by putting forward something that might be small yet novel that adds value to a task or an activity.

Let me distinguish with an example. The renowned chef Heston Blumenthal is adept at developing complicated, original recipes and food concepts that make you scratch your head and ask, 'How on earth did he come up with that?' That is the sign of a creative genius at play.

Now I wouldn't describe my mother as a creative genius in the kitchen, or generally a creative person full stop, but she does show creativity when it comes to modifying recipes or putting her own slant on a classic dish. These novel modifications may not seem creative to a professional chef, but to those around her she is admired for her creative touches in the kitchen. She makes the most amazing healthy muffins where she has taken a standard recipe and, using her creativity, substituted ingredients or added others to create a treat that is delicious and loved by all members of the family. I am not sure any one of us would have come up with the substitute ideas she has, but they work marvellously.

This goes to show how simple creativity with purpose can lead to enormous benefits for those around you. It highlights how you don't have to be a creative genius to be creative. This view of creativity challenges the view that it is an innate quality. As discussed in Chapter 4, anyone with the right mindset (willing to work hard, experiment, learn and persist through failure) can be creative. We need to see that creativity can emerge anywhere, whether it be cooking up a storm in the kitchen, playing games with the kids, or simply collaborating with your team.

I worked with a team a few years back where I wouldn't have identified any of the members as creative in their own right; however, together they were fantastic. In group conversations characterised by openness, vulnerability and curiosity, they created an energy where creativity emerged. They were able to feed off each other and generate ideas that were novel and effective. My sense is that they wouldn't have been able to do that as effectively by themselves.

Creativity is an important tool in our kit bag for responding nimbly to complexity in the workplace. One of the best responses to complexity is running multiple experiments to identify what helps us to move forward and what doesn't. Multiple experiments require us to use our creativity to put forward unique ideas and new ways to test them.

One final point I want to make about creativity is that the more time you spend honing your craft, whatever that might be, the more opportunity you have to be creative. For most of us, creativity doesn't come in the form of an innate talent, but in deliberate practice and time spent getting good at something. If you have spent time developing your practice or craft, then the likelihood is that has become second nature to you. You don't have to think about it as much. This frees you up to think about how you might improve or challenge the status quo with a unique idea. It can reduce your conservatism to take risks.

Over the years I have run thousands of workshops. Due to that experience, nothing really fazes me about designing or delivering a workshop. If a client came to me with a significant change on the day, I know I could be creative in how I manage that situation. What allows me to do that is the fact that running the workshop is a micro-skill I have developed, allowing me space to think creatively about solutions that are unique and add value. Therefore, I know I can be creative in small ways when it comes to my area of expertise.

Ideas for unleashing your creativity

Create time and space to feed your inspiration and creative juices

If I want to be creative in some aspects of my work (such as writing this book), I go down to my beach house on the Surf Coast of Victoria. I write with the sea in the background, I go for a walk or a bike ride to simply get out in nature. If I am too busy in my life, I find my creative juices are zapped. You don't need to have a beach house, but you do need to create space and time. So find what helps you to think. It might be hiking, talking to others, meditating or swimming. The most important thing is that you create space and time to allow for creativity to emerge. It is unlikely to emerge if you are busy being busy, or wasting your free time on passive activities like watching Netflix or browsing social media.

Learn to experiment

Experimentation is an important part of the creative process. It's about trying things, following hunches, learning from your experiments and refining. Creativity is not about getting it right the first time. When my mum experimented with her fruit muffins it took a few attempts before she and others felt happy with them. Experimentation requires us to lean into vulnerability and fail safely. Our learning leads us to greater creativity. Even creative geniuses are experimenters. If you want to know more about experimentation, I refer you to Chapter 23.

Surround yourself with creative people and people who think differently to you

One of the experiments I am undertaking as I write this chapter is a month-long co-working and co-living retreat in Bali. On the retreat there are diverse people with different creative backgrounds. Backgrounds that I have had little exposure to, including social media, videography, photography and floral design. Some of them are the best at what they do internationally. As I observe their skills, ideas and experiments it allows my own creative process to emerge. I have been able to get more creative about the design of my website and the launch of my book. Creativity can come from surrounding yourself with people who think differently to you. These differences, if you are open and curious, can energise and stimulate your ideas and thoughts.

CHAPTER 36

Decision Agility

Every day, from the moment we get up to the time we go to bed, we are making decisions and choices. Some are relatively inconsequential, such as which café you get your morning coffee from, or which glass of wine you have with a friend after work. Others are more challenging, such as whether you make a radical change to your pricing strategy, or whether to have children or buy that house. The ability to get the balance right between responsiveness and quality in decision making is important at both an individual and an organisational level. Poor decision making can be devastating to organisations.

In 2012, Kodak filed for bankruptcy after being in business for over 130 years. They had missed the boat when it came to digital technology even though one of the employees, Steve Sasson, invented a prototype of the first digital camera[49]. The decision to not pursue this technology was primarily made on the basis that Kodak's revenue was in film processing, and that this technology would cannibalise their earnings. I am a lover of Netflix, and as part of my research for this book, I read that the CEO of Netflix Reed Hastings went to Blockbuster in 2000 to sell his business for $50 million. Blockbuster said no and today no longer exists, whilst Netflix has market capitalisation of nearly

$50 billion USD[50]. Poor decisions and choices are costly!

There are many factors that lead to poor decision making. The two major ones I see are not understanding context, and not managing cognitive biases in the decision-making process.

Let's look at the importance of context. At an individual level, people are praised for being decisive. You know those people who are cool and calm under pressure, firm and strong and quick to act. That type of decision making appeals to people and is an antidote to 'paralysis by analysis'. In a world of predictability and order, it is much easier to make quick decisions. However, as environments get more complex, quick decisive action may prove problematic. It is why we must understand context if we want to be a better decision maker. In Chapter 8 I discussed one way to understand your context through Heifetz and Linsky's work on adaptive and technical challenges. Understanding which challenges you are facing can influence your approach to decision making. When you are facing technical challenges within a stable environment, with a higher degree of predictability and a likely known cause and effect, then decision making can be based on past experiences, evidence and expertise. In most cases, in this type of environment, there is usually one right answer.

However, if you are facing an adaptive challenge in a complex environment, where there is unpredictability and where cause and effect are often unknown, then quick decisions may result in unintended consequences. In this complex environment, staying openminded, exploring options and solutions through experimentation, and knowing that there may be no right answer is often the best approach to decision making. Unfortunately, we often have a bias for action and a need to restore certainty and order, and this can lead to making ineffective decisions.

The second main contributor to poor decision making is

cognitive bias. A 2010 McKinsey study[51] ('The Case for Behavioural Strategy') of more than 1000 major business investments showed that when organisations worked at reducing the effect of bias in their decision-making processes, they achieved returns up to seven percentage points higher. In Chapter 11, I discussed the importance of understanding cognitive biases. Unfortunately, knowing your cognitive biases doesn't mean you can necessarily eliminate them in yourself. You have a better chance of spotting biases in others. You can, however, reduce bias through a rigorous decision-making process. A couple of biases to take note of are overconfidence or optimism bias, and confirmation bias.

Overconfidence bias refers to a situation where people's confidence in their judgements and knowledge is higher than the accuracy of these judgements. We can have a rose-coloured view of things based on past experiences, our expertise, our organisational position or our past success. For example, I might think I am pretty good at picking shares because in the past I have been able to do this well. However, this overconfidence can lead me to focus on my ability, rather than luck or context, such as market conditions. It is this overconfidence that leads to poor strategic decisions, such as those made by Kodak and Blockbuster. It can also lead to people making risky decisions about experimenting with recreational drugs ('nothing will happen to me') or driving after a couple of drinks because they consider themselves a good driver. Don't get me wrong. Confidence in decision making is important. We expect that from people who are exercising leadership. However, if we are *over*confident, we can disregard important information and data, and end up making poor decisions.

The second bias that impacts decision making is **confirmation bias**. Confirmation bias, described in more detail in Chapter 11, is where our brain seeks out and favours information that confirms our beliefs and assumptions (our mental model) or ignores information that contradicts them. If we decide that a particular path is the right one to take, then we will look for data to support the decision we've made, often discounting other important data. We can unconsciously ignore alternatives as they don't fit the way we see the world. Confirmation bias can influence decisions around strategy, selecting a person for promotion, or who gets your vote on election day.

One way to help you manage both overconfidence bias and confirmation bias is to involve others in your decision-making process. It is easier to spot the bias of someone else than it is to spot your own. I describe how you might do that in the ideas below.

Making efficient decisions is important, but making the right decisions considering context and our own biases is vital if we are to respond effectively in an increasingly complex world.

Ideas for cultivating decision agility

Involve others in your decision making (Part 1)

The first way to involve others is to encourage dissenting views. We often shut down voices that disagree with our approach or decisions. It is important that we value the dissenting voices and embrace the 'no'. We can do that by exploring the dissenting opinion and trying to see things from someone else's perspective. Dissenting voices can help overcome groupthink, where people are encouraged to stay in unity on particular decisions. You might allocate someone the role of devil's advocate and get them to point out the shortfalls in an approach or a decision. You could also surround yourself in general by people who think differently to you. Colliding perspectives is a useful ingredient in effective decision making. It helps you overcome your own personal biases.

Involve others in your decision making (Part 2)

The second way you can involve others is to encourage availability of information. Daniel Kahneman, Dan Lovallo and Olivier Sibony, in their 2011 *Harvard Business Review* article, 'The Big Idea: Before You Make that Big Decision'[52], on decision making, encourage the decision maker to ask people, 'If I had to make this decision again in 12 months' time, what additional information would I want, and can I get more of that information and data now?' This moves the decision maker away from existing information that might confirm an existing belief, to data that may not have been thought of or encouraged.

Generate multiple options

Decision making is often only as good as the options available. If we have a narrow range of alternatives or options, then we are limited in the decision we can make. I am not talking about having too many options, as that can lead to 'paralysis by analysis'. We are talking about moving beyond one or two options to three or four. Increasing your options by this small amount can lead to better decision making. Increasing options can be done by involving others, exploring multiple alternatives to a situation, using 'both/and' thinking (Chapter 8) or simply considering the opposite of what you plan to do. This might generate a further palatable option that you hadn't considered.

Final Thoughts

In writing and launching a book, you open yourself up to feedback – both positive and negative. No doubt there will be some people who love this book and find it useful, and there will be others who may not. I think at times the procrastination in writing was caused by the fear of what people might think. However, for me to demonstrate my own agility and grow as a person, I needed to let go of attaching my ego to what people might think about the book. I came to the conclusion that, if it makes a difference to one person, then it is a worthwhile endeavour. The writing and launch of this book has already made a difference – to me! It inspired me to think about my own agility, and whether I am practicing what I preach. This is one of the core values I hold dearly in the work I am doing. If I am asking my clients to think, engage and act differently, then I need to ensure that I am doing the same.

When I started writing this book, I realised that whilst I was making personal progress in many cases, I was falling short in others. I noticed that I wasn't practicing self-care. I was doing work I wasn't enjoying, and I felt stagnant. I needed to make an intervention and run a series of experiments that would help me grow as a person, and bring the fun back into my life. After all, if I wasn't growing and having fun, then how could I truly be of service to my clients?

So I decided to step well outside my comfort zone. I have

taken six months off (December 2018 to May 2019) to practice self-care and to run a series of experiments. Some of the activities and experiments I am exploring (or have explored) include singing lessons, improvisation comedy, attending a yoga and meditation retreat, living and working in Bali at a co-working retreat, braving a stand-up comedy gig, and surrounding myself with people who think differently to me. As I write this, I know there will be other experiments that stretch and challenge me. Even the decision to take six months off is outside my comfort zone, as I love my work and don't like to disappoint my clients! Fortunately, they have been very supportive and understand why I am doing this. I am writing a blog, documenting my progress and what I have learnt. If you are interested in joining me on my journey, please head to cultivateagility.com.

I am also keen to get your feedback, both positive and negative, on this book. I would love to know how it impacted you or what might have been different for you. If there are additional ideas that you think would be worthwhile including in another edition, please feel free to contact me at andrew@agilityconsulting.com.au.

Thank you for taking the time to read this book, and I wish you well on your development journey.

Andrew Williams
June 2019
www.cultivateagility.com

Acknowledgements

American journalist and novelist Gene Fowler once said, 'Writing is easy. All you do is stare at a blank sheet of paper until drops of blood form on your forehead.' At times this felt very true for me. The writing of a book is never an easy process, but it becomes easier when you have people to support you.

I firstly have to acknowledge the thousands of clients are I have worked with either in a workshop, speaking or coaching capacity. They have inspired this book, and I continue to learn from them every day. My profession is a privilege and I admire the courage and the commitment of my clients to do the real work.

I would also like to acknowledge a range of practitioners who have influenced my development and my thinking around cultivating leadership agility. Some have had a direct influence, such as Ron Heifetz, Marty Linsky and Bob Kegan from Harvard, and Ed O'Malley and the team at the Kansas Leadership Center (KLC). The work of the KLC is truly inspiring. There are also those who have had an indirect influence, such as Dave Snowden, Mike Lombardo, Bob Eichinger, Bill Joiner, Otto Scharmer, Jill Hufnagel, Nick Petrie and Jennifer Garvey Berger.

I want to give a shout out to my AGSM colleagues at the University of New South Wales Business School, particularly Patrick Sharry, who has been a brilliant support to me in my own development and the best colleague to collaborate with. I have also met many wonderful practitioners at workshops and conferences around the world. I have learnt so much from them. A special shout out to Gina Jackson and Susan Sturm.

I have a lovely set of friends who have been on the journey with me and I want to thank them for their encouragement and support. It means so much to me.

This book would never have got to this stage if it wasn't for the amazing work done by my editors, Rebecca Hamilton and Ann Wilson from Independent Ink. Writing can be a lonely business but having the support of Bec and Ann in the editing process helped me enormously. They managed to keep my voice and make the book readable and accessible. They challenged me in the most supportive way. I cannot speak highly enough of them.

Finally, to my parents, Ron and Heather, who set me on this development path many years ago, thank you so much. I love you, and I am who I am because of you.

About the Author

Andrew Williams is the Founder and Managing Director of Agility Consulting Group. He has been an Adjunct Faculty at the Australia Graduate School of Management at the University of NSW for over 10 years where he facilitates executive programs in adaptive leadership, leadership agility and personal growth.

In June 2017, Andrew won the prestigious AGSM executive education outstanding faculty award. This award recognises those who have made outstanding contributions to the quality of participant learning and the quality of participant experience in executive education.

Andrew is a graduate of The Art and Practice of Leadership Development at the Harvard Kennedy School of Government which has enabled him to work with teams in the area of adaptive leadership and transformational change. He is also a practitioner in Case-in-Point teaching methodology and was certified as a Master Practitioner in this powerful methodology through the Kansas Leadership Centre. He uses this form of teaching methodology with intact teams, leadership cohorts and in programs with AGSM clients.

In his work Andrew regularly works with senior teams to help them work through issues that are important to them. He is able to facilitate dialogue, help groups anchor to purpose and hold up a mirror to enable groups to see how their dynamics are helping or hindering their ability to make progress. Andrew enjoys challenging a group and creates a safe holding space to enable that to happen.

Andrew's impressive client list covers industries such as Banking & Finance, Government, Telecommunications, Energy, Retail, FMCG, Insurance, Construction, Professional Services, and Media & Publishing. Andrew has worked in a number of countries across his career and is passionate about helping any individual or team in any location.

Andrew is an **outstanding coach, workshop facilitator, speaker and educator** bringing a unique blend of energy, humour, creativity and learning to every program and presentation.

In his spare time Andrew, enjoys the theatre, running, entertaining, collecting wine, domestic and international travel and for his sins follows Carlton in the AFL.

Reference List

1 Axon, L., Freidman, E. & Jordan K. (2015) *Leading Now: Critical Capabilities for a Complex World* Harvard Business School Publishing

2 Axon, L., Freidman, E. & Jordan K. (2015) *Leading Now: Critical Capabilities for a Complex World* Harvard Business School Publishing p 6

3 Garvey Berger, J. & Fitzgerald, C. (2015) *Coaching for an Increasingly Complex World* Cultivating Leadership White Paper

4 Kolb, D.A., Rubin, I.M. & Osland J. (1991) *Organizational Behavior: An Experiential Approach.* Prentice Hall International

5 Heifitz, R.A. & Linsky, M.L. (2002) *Leadership on the Line* Harvard Business School Publishing

6 Dweck, C.S. (2006) *Mindset* Ballantine Books

7 Dweck, C.S. (2006) *Mindset* p 39 Ballantine Books

8 Heifitz, R.A. & Linsky, M.L. (2002) *Leadership on the Line* Harvard Business School Publishing

9 Cognitive Edge (Producer) 2018 Cynefin Foundations Online Course

10 Wedell-Wedellsborg, T. (HBR Jan/Feb 2017) *Are You Solving the Right Problems* Harvard Business School Publishing

11 For more detail on making interpretations see Heifitz, R., Grashow, A. & Linsky, M (2009) *The practice of Adaptive Leadership* Cambridge Leadership Associates

12 Senge, P., Ross, R., Smith, B., Roberts, C. & Kleiner A (1994) *The Fifth Discipline: The Art and Practice of Learning Organisations* Nicholas Brearley Publishing

13 Collins, J. & Porras J.I. (1994) *Built to Last* William Collins Publishing

14 Johnson, B. (1992) *Polarity management: Identifying and managing unsolvable problems* Human Resource Development Press

15 Gino, F. (HBR Sept/Oct 2018) *The Business Case for Curiosity* Harvard Business School Publishing

16 Bennis, W.G. & Thomas, R.J. (2002) *Geeks & Geezers: How Era, Values and Defining Moments Shape Leaders* Harvard Business School Press

17 Bennis, W.G. & Thomas, R.J. (2002) *Geeks & Geezers: How Era, Values and Defining Moments Shape Leaders* P 20 Harvard Business School Press

18 Brown, S. & Vaughan, C. (2010) *Play: How it Shapes the Brain, Opens the Imagination and Invigorates the Soul* Penguin Random House

19 Kahneman, D. (2011) *Thinking Fast and Slow* Farrar, Straus and Giroux Publishing

20 Senge, P., Ross, R., Smith, B., Roberts, C. & Kleiner A (1994) *The Fifth Discipline: The Art and Practice of Learning Organisations* Nicholas Brearley Publishing

21 Hill, L.A., Brandeau, G., Truelove, E. & Lineback, K. (2014) *Collective Genius: The Art and Practice of Leading Innovation* p65 Harvard Business Review Press

22 Heifitz, R.A. & Linsky, M.L. (2002) *Leadership on the Line* Harvard Business School Publishing

23 For more detail on giving the work back see Heifitz, R., Grashow, A. & Linsky, M (2009) *The practice of Adaptive Leadership* Cambridge Leadership Associates

24 Bock, L. (Speaker). (2016, December 21). *How to be More Productive* [Audio podcast]. Retrieved from http://itunes.apple.com

25 Edmondson, A.C. (2012) *Teaming: How Organizations Learn, Innovate and Compete in the Knowledge Economy* p 118 Harvard Business School

26 Duhhig, C. '*What Google Learned From Its Quest to Build the Perfect Team*' New York Times 25 February 2016, viewed [12 March 2019] https://www.nytimes.com/2016/02/28/magazine/what-google-learned-from-its-quest-to-build-the-perfect-team.html

27 This an excellent book to help leverage the power of teams in organisations

28 Brown, B. (2010, June). Brene Bown: *The Power of Vulnerability* [Video file]. Retrieved from https://www.ted.com/talks/brene brown_the_power_of_vulnerability

29 Rosenberg, M. (Speaker) (2011, July). *Non Violent Communication with Marshall Rosenberg: An Introduction* [Video file]. Retrieved from https://www.youtube.com/watch?v=DgaeHeIL39Y&t=190s

30 Botsman, R. 2017 *Who Can You Trust: How Technology Brought Us Together and Why It Might Drive Us Apart* Public Affairs Books

31 Krznaric, R. (2014) *Empathy; Why It Matters, And How To Get It* Rider

32 Krznaric, R. (2014) *Empathy; Why It Matters, And How To Get It* p 11 Rider

33 Hill, L.A., Brandeau, G., Truelove, E. & Lineback, K. (2014) *Collective Genius: The Art and Practice of Leading Innovation* p138 Harvard Business Review Press

34 Brown, B. (2010, June). Brene Bown: *The Power of Vulnerability* [Video file]. Retrieved from https://www.ted.com/talks/brene brown_the_power_of_vulnerability

35 Brown, B. (2012) *Daring Greatly; How the Courage to Be Vulnerable Transforms the Way we Live, Love, Parent and Lead* Avery

36 Brown, B. Daring Greatly; *How the Courage to Be Vulnerable Transforms the Way we Live, Love, Parent and Lead* P33 Avery

37 Issacs, W. (1999) *Dialogue and The Art of Thinking* Together Doubleday

38 Cohen, A.R. & Bradford, D.L. (2017) *Influence without Authority* 3rd Ed Wiley

39 ThemPra Social Pedagogy C.I.C., 'The Learning Zone Model', [Viewed May 02 2019] http://www.thempra.org.uk/social-pedagogy/key-concepts-in-social-pedagogy/the-learning-zone-model/

40 Sull, D. & Eisenhardt, K. M. ((2015) *Simple Rules: How To Thrive IN A Complex World* Houghton Mifflin Harcourt

41 Sinek, S, S. (2009, September). *Simon Sinek: How Great Leaders Inspire Action* [Video file]. Retrieved from https://www.ted.com/talks/simon_sinek_how_great_leaders_inspire_action

42 Sinek, S. (2009) *Start with Why; How Great Leaders Inspire Everyone To Take Action* Portfolio penguin

43 Ludeman, K. & Erlandson, E. (2006) *Alpha Male Syndrome* Harvard Business Review Press

44 Brittain Leslie, J. & Peterson, M. J. (2011) *The benchmarks Source Book Three Decades of Related Research* CCL Press

45 For further discussion on learning from experiences I refer you to the 70/20/10 concept of development

46 Goldsmith, M. (Retrieved 13 March 2019). *Marshall Goldsmith/ Feedfoward* [Video file]. Retrieved http://marshallgoldsmithfeedforward.com/html/FeedForward-Tool.htm

47 Kegan, R. & Laskow Lahey, L. (2009) *Immunity to Change; How Overcome It And Unlock The Potential In Yourself And Your Organization* Harvard Business School Publishing

48 Watkins, M. D. (2013) *The First 90 Days: Critical Success Strategies for New Leaders at All Levels* Expanded Edition Harvard Business Review Press

49 Harvey, I., (July 25 2016) Steve Sasson invented the first digital camera but was forced to keep it hidden [Viewed March 12 2019] https://www.thevintagenews.com/2016/07/25/steve-sasson-invented-the-first-digital-camera-in-1975-but-was-forced-to-keep-it-hidden/

50 Chong, C., (July 18 2015) Blockbuster's CEO once passed up a chance to buy Netflix for only $50 million [Viewed March 13 2019] https://www.businessinsider.com.au/blockbuster-ceo-passed-up-chance-to-buy-netflix-for-50-million-2015-7

51 Lovallo, D. & Sibony, O. (March 2010) The Case for Behavioural Strategy McKinsey Quarterly

52 Kahneman, D., Lovallo, D. & Sibony, O. (HBR June 2011) The Big Idea: Before You Make that Big Decision Harvard Business School Publishing

www.ingramcontent.com/pod-product-compliance
Lightning Source LLC
Chambersburg PA
CBHW071203210326
41597CB00016B/1652